The Clash of Globalizations

ANTHEM FRONTIERS OF GLOBAL POLITICAL ECONOMY

The **Anthem Frontiers of Global Political Economy** series seeks
to trigger and attract new thinking in global political economy, with particular
reference to the prospects of emerging markets and developing countries. Written by
renowned scholars from different parts of the world, books in this series provide historical,
analytical and empirical perspectives on national economic strategies and processes, the
implications of global and regional economic integration, the changing nature of the
development project, and the diverse global-to-local forces that drive change.
Scholars featured in the series extend earlier economic insights to
provide fresh interpretations that allow new understandings
of contemporary economic processes.

Series Editors

Kevin Gallagher – Boston University, USA
Jayati Ghosh – Jawaharlal Nehru University, India

Editorial Board

Stephanie Blankenburg – School of Oriental and African Studies (SOAS), UK
Ha-Joon Chang – University of Cambridge, UK
Wan-Wen Chu – RCHSS, Academia Sinica, Taiwan
Léonce Ndikumana – University of Massachusetts-Amherst, USA
Alica Puyana Mutis – Facultad Latinoamericana de Ciencias Sociales (FLASCO-México), Mexico
Matías Vernengo – Banco Central de la República Argentina, Argentina
Robert Wade – London School of Economics and Political Science (LSE), UK
Yu Yongding – Chinese Academy of Social Sciences (CASS), China

The Clash of Globalizations

Essays on the Political Economy of Trade and Development Policy

Kevin P. Gallagher

ANTHEM PRESS
LONDON · NEW YORK · DELHI

Anthem Press
An imprint of Wimbledon Publishing Company
www.anthempress.com

This edition first published in UK and USA 2014
by ANTHEM PRESS
75–76 Blackfriars Road, London SE1 8HA, UK
or PO Box 9779, London SW19 7ZG, UK
and
244 Madison Ave #116, New York, NY 10016, USA

First published in hardback by Anthem Press in 2013

British Library Cataloguing-in-Publication Data
A catalogue record for this book is available from the British Library.

Library of Congress Cataloging-in-Publication Data
The Library of Congress has catalogued the hardcover edition as follows:
Gallagher, Kevin, 1968–
The clash of globalizations : essays on the political economy of trade and development
policy / Kevin P. Gallagher.
pages cm
Includes bibliographical references and index.
ISBN-13: 978-0-85728-327-6 (hardback : alk. paper)
ISBN-10: 0-85728-327-8 (hardback : alk. paper)
1. International trade. 2. Economic development. 3. Development economics.
4. Globalization. 5. Developing countries–Economic policy. I. Title.
HF1379.G347 2013
382.01–dc23
2013012695

ISBN-13: 978 1 78308 342 8 (Pbk)
ISBN-10: 1 78308 342 5 (Pbk)

Cover photograph © Agência Brasil, licensed under Creative Commons.

This title is also available as an ebook.

This book is dedicated to Alice Amsden

CONTENTS

PREFACE AND ACKNOWLEDGMENTS

Fifteen years ago I had the privilege of being a student of the late Alice Amsden. We were reading her working manuscript for what was to become her opus book, *The Rise of the Rest: Challenges to the West from Late Industrializing Economies*. That book showed how, borrowing from the West, the most successful developing countries mixed government policy with market forces to transform their economies from rural ones to global export powerhouses. Her book echoed and was echoed by superscholars such as Peter Evans, Dani Rodrik and Robert Wade to name but a few. I dedicate this book to Alice's memory. She passed away, too early, while the manuscript was under preparation.

At the time of Amsden's class I was writing a dissertation on the United States' trade policy, looking specifically at the North American Free Trade Agreement (NAFTA). Week after week as we analyzed scholarship about these policies that were so successful in East Asia and beyond I kept saying to myself, "Hey, you couldn't do that under NAFTA."

Over the course of the first decade of the new century then, while working on a different core research agenda I slowly chipped away conducting in-depth analyses examining the extent to which emerging market and developing nations could use specific policies that had been used by others. At first, such analyses were often engagements with the legal literature, pinpointing policies and examining whether new laws and codes would still permit them. Chapters 2, 3 and 4 of this book are updated versions of those attempts to make sense of the seemingly conflicting regimes of national development policy and the trading system. I also edited a book in 2005 titled *Putting Development First: The Need for Policy Space in the WTO and International Financial Institutions*.

As this work started to gain attention, in both policy and academic circles, I started to encounter the following question: if these policies are so bad then why are nations signing on to them? This set of questions led to an engagement with the literature in international political economy. Robert Wade, who contributed a landmark article to that 2005 book, put me in touch with Kenneth Shadlen, also at the London School of Economics.

Ken's scholarship sparked the thinking that went into Chapters 5 and 6 of this volume. Chapter 5 examines the politics of the WTO around these issues, and Chapter 6 confronts that question head on and explains why some nations have signed trade agreements that run counter to their long-run economic interests.

The chapters in this book then are revised and slightly updated versions of articles written during the first decade of this century – and they examine the political economy of trade and development policy at the turn of the century. In addition to thanking the scholars just mentioned for their inspiration, curiosity and guidance, I also thank the following journals and institutes for publishing work that at the time seemed out of the ordinary. Earlier versions of this work have been published in *Review of International Political Economy*, *New Political Economy*, *Global Policy* and the *Denver Journal of International Law and Policy*. In addition, the International Centre for Trade and Sustainable Development in Geneva and also published versions of some of these chapters as discussion papers.

I am particularly indebted to Rachel Denae Thrasher, who coauthored what is now Chapter 4 with me. Rachel is a lawyer and teaming up with her helped me really understand trade law and its application. What I learned from her helped guide me through other topics later on.

As time went by, with the encouragement of others I came to realize that these articles and studies added up to a bigger picture. That is what has led to collecting them all in this book. Chapter 1 pulls all the books findings and political economy insights into a whole and envelops the volume. The next three chapters are analyses that examine the extent to which nations have surrendered policy space for various development policies through their trade commitments. Chapter 2 examines the ability to regulate cross-border finance, Chapter 3 discusses sovereign debt restructuring and Chapter 4 (with Rachel) examines industrial policy. Chapters 5 and 6 look at the political economy dynamics that led to those outcomes. Chapter 7 looks to the future and presents the elements of a more development-friendly trading system.

I have already thanked Alice Amsden, Peter Evans, Dani Rodrik and Robert Wade for their early work that inspired mine, and Kenneth Shadlen and Rachel Thrasher for helping me think about and analyze that earlier work in a twenty-first-century context. There are many more who I have known, worked with and learned from on these issues, including Nagesh Kumar, Ha-Joon Chang, Alisa DiCaprio, Ricardo Melendez-Ortiz, Werner Corrales, Martin Khor, Joel Trachtman, Lori Wallach, Sarah Anderson and many others.

Much of this work was supported by the Global Development and Environment (GDAE) institute from grants by the Rockefeller Brothers Fund and the C. S. Mott Foundation. Frank Ackerman and Timothy Wise at GDAE have been core partners and friends throughout this work. I coauthored many spinoffs from this work for policymakers with each of these men. At the supporting foundations I particularly thank Michael Conroy, Thomas Kruse, Sandra Smithey, Amy Shannon, Ed Miller and Kay Treakel, as well as Carolyne Deere from the Rockefeller Foundation.

In 2004 I began working as a professor at Boston University full-time. The university, and the Department of International Relations in particular, has been a very supportive environment for this work. I especially thank my graduate students who have taken IR 789: Globalization, Development, and Governance with me. Until recently this class exclusively focused on trade policy and development and much of my writing on this came out of or was tried out on that class.

At Boston University I am a faculty fellow at the Pardee Center for the Study of the Longer-Run Future. The center's former director, Adil Najam, encouraged me to establish the Global Economic Governance Initiative there, which I now run. The Pardee Center has provided financial and many other forms of support for this and subsequent support. Support for which I am very grateful.

I thank Tej Sood, Rob Reddick and the whole team at Anthem Press for their enthusiasm about this book. Indeed, at their request I have Indian economist and friend Jayati Ghosh as coeditor of an exciting new book series, Anthem Frontiers of Global Political Economy, that this book will fall under.

The core of my life's inspiration is my family. Kelly, Theo and Estelle, thank you for giving my life, and work, so much purpose.

LIST OF TABLES, FIGURES AND BOXES

Tables

Figures

Boxes

Chapter 1

INTRODUCING THE CLASH OF GLOBALIZATIONS

By the turn of the century global trade talks seemed destined to raise the roof of low politics, where international political economy has long been relegated. Large street protests accompanied negotiations, heads of state and hopefuls discussed trade in public and on campaign trails at least as much as security, and the media followed it all in paparazzi-like fashion.

What a difference a decade makes. By 2013 global trade talks at the World Trade Organization (WTO) had come to a complete standstill. None of the major players – the United States, Europe, emerging markets or global justice protestors – had been willing to significantly engage since at best 2008.

For the first time in the history of global trade negotiations, rather than a clash among Western interests, deadlock among negotiators has been a function of a clash between industrialized countries and developing countries with newfound economic power. The seeds of this clash can be found in the Uruguay Round (1986 to 1994), where a deal was struck whereby the industrialized nations traded market access to their large and growing economies for domestic regulatory changes in the developing world in the areas of investment law, intellectual property, services and beyond (Narlikar 2003).

This book collects a number of essays that ask the following questions: To what extent is the global trading regime reducing the ability of nation-states to pursue policies for financial stability and economic growth, and what political factors explain such changes in policy space over time, across different types of trade treaties and across nations?

The essays in this book show that there was a significant constraining of policy space under the Uruguay Round, but there is still a significant amount of room to maneuver for developing countries. However, many regional and bilateral deals, especially with the United States, severely restrict the ability of developing nations to amply deploy a range of development strategies for stability, growth and development.

In the latest round of WTO talks, many emerging market and developing economies saw the benefits of further global trade liberalization as relatively small, and the costs as being quite significant in terms of the loss of "policy space" they see as necessary to develop their economies or stay in office. The WTO's standstill can thus be seen as a relative success from their standpoint. The WTO as an institution for disputes and monitoring remains intact, but it does not further impede regulatory changes at the domestic level that are politically and sometimes economically costly. And with respect to intellectual property rules and public health at least, the developing world has been able to gain back some policy space.

Such findings lead me to characterize twenty-first-century trade politics, at the global level at least, as a "clash of globalizations" whereby developed nations see it as in their interest to promote a global trade regime that helps solidify and expand their current (or static) comparative advantage in capital and knowledge-intensive goods and services. Many developing nations see it as in their interest to build upon their current comparative advantage in primary commodities and light manufacturing and expand into new, more value-added intensive areas where someday they *might* have a comparative advantage.

The key difference between the recent round of talks – referred to as the Doha Round – and past rounds, is that developing nations have had the economic and political power to refuse industrialized country proposals and to put forth an alternative set of negotiating demands that industrialized countries have to take seriously. Economic power of course isn't the only factor that explains the difference, but it is key among a confluence of factors that also include institutional structure, domestic politics, currency fluctuations and ideas about globalization.

These two approaches to globalization can each be seen as rational. Each has been successful in maintaining or raising living standards for their respective citizens. This at least partly explains why the WTO is in deadlock, why the WTO in relative terms still grants developing nations relatively more policy space (than North–South bilateral investment treaties (BITs) and preferential trade agreements (PTAs)) to pursue their own development strategies, and why regional and bilateral trade treaties have proliferated to such a degree that they may threaten the global trade regime – a regime that has just started to generate more equal outcomes.

Varieties of Globalization and the Trade Regime

During the postwar era many countries deployed a variant of what John Ruggie (1983) called "embedded liberalism" – global trade and investment liberalization "embedded" within national-level institutional frameworks to promote domestic economic growth and financial stability. As is the case in the industrialized world, where there are numerous "varieties" of industrial capitalism, there have been varying regimes of embeddedness across the developing world as well. The key difference between embedded liberalism in the industrialized countries and in the developing world is that, in the industrialized North, the interest was to *maintain* a high level of industrialization and stability, whereas, in the developing world, the goal was to *obtain* a satisfactory standard of living and stability for their populations. As countries seek to re-embed markets in the twenty-first century, these different goals persist. Such goals translate into different sets of interests and negotiation stances in trade politics.

Similar to the experiences of industrialized countries, embedded liberalism lost momentum in the developing world beginning in the 1980s (more so in Latin American than in East Asia). For close to two decades the "Washington Consensus" approach characterized much of developing country economic policy – an approach that stresses the liberalization of trade and investment alongside the general reduction of the role of the state in economic affairs. Though many nations still espouse the Washington Consensus approach, some nations such as Brazil, South Africa, India, China, Malaysia and others began to re-embed markets with state activity to diversify economies and reach global markets with the goal of raising living standards. These nations represent a variety of globalization that has not received much attention in academic and policy circles. Indeed, some treatments of China and Brazil attribute the growth of those nations to "globalizing" although both nations have done so with a mix of industrial policy and state-facilitated macromanagement for development.

There is an enormous literature in political economy circles known as the "varieties of capitalism" literature. The originators of this body of work, Peter Hall and David Soskice (2001), focused mainly on the West and keenly categorized industrial capitalism as having "liberal market economies" that are more market-based (US, UK) and "coordinated market economies" where the state plays a stronger role in coordinating market activity (Scandinavia, Germany, Japan).

The core of the "varieties of capitalism" literature is largely focused on varieties of industrial capitalism in the West. However, a related discourse has been occurring among political economists of economic development, albeit under a different guise (standout exceptions are Schneider 2009 and Breslin 2007). In the 1980s and the 1990s there was significant attention paid by political economists to the role of the state in economic development (the classic summary volume is Woo-Cumings 1999). This literature, which focused on East Asian nations beginning with Japan, as well as some Latin American nations (especially Brazil and Mexico in the early 1980s), suggested that:

In states that were late to industrialize, the state itself led the industrialization drive, that is, it took on developmental functions.

These two differing orientations toward private economic activities, the
regulatory orientation and the developmental orientation, produced
two different kinds of business–government relationships. The United
States is a good example of a state in which the regulatory orientation
predominates, whereas Japan is a good example of a state in which
the developmental orientation predominates. A regulatory, or market-
rational, state concerns itself with the forms and procedures – the rules,
if you will – of economic competition, but it does not concern itself with
substantive matters. (Johnson 1982, 19)

The two literatures have never been neatly knit together, but a global look at
economies and the role of the state would put many developmental states into
a separate "variety" of capitalism. In today's light, it should be stressed that
globalization of trade, or at least export orientation, was the key goal of the most
successful developmental states in Asia. And that the most significant emerging
market players in the WTO and beyond are at least hybrid developmental
states. While many of those nations that were developmental states in the past
are not so today, such as South Korea, a new crop has arisen. Today, China is
the exemplar developmental state, and Brazil, South Africa and India today
are lesser variants as well. It should also be noted that developmentalism is
not simply a state-centric "decision" but the outcome of a political process.
In the case of Brazil, for instance, decision makers in the government who
subscribe to a more developmentalist perspective are bolstered by (or in office
because of) a domestic industrial or service class that cannot yet compete with
its industrialized country counterparts.

This "variety" of globalization – one where developing countries seek to
integrate with the world economy in order to achieve a higher standard of
living by having the state play a key role diversifying their product and export
base – stands in contrast with the liberal market economy model and to some
extent with the coordinated market economy models found in the West. In
parallel to the description of embedded liberalism above, Western nations seek
to maintain and expand global markets for those sectors where they enjoy an
existing (or static) comparative advantage. Developing countries, at least some
of them, seek to change the underlying structure of their economies over time
and someday gain a comparative advantage in a broader set of sectors. The
state may play a key role in such diversification.

What is clear is that liberal market economies pursue the most liberal
trading arrangements, as do coordinated market economies from Europe,
though to a lesser extent (see Gallagher and Thrasher 2010). Western
nations are seeking to consolidate and expand their current comparative
advantages on a global level. Let us call them "consolidating globalizers."

Meanwhile, poor and middle-income countries in other regions have a different variant of globalizing capitalism. They are "developmental globalizers" that are still working the right mix of markets and states in order to achieve higher standards of living.

Emerging market and developing countries have been growing faster than their industrialized counterparts since the turn of the century. The developing world "took off" in terms of gross domestic product (GDP) per capita growth from 2000 to 2008, then dipped as the industrialized world did due to the financial crisis. Developing countries grew 4.7 percent per annum in per capita terms, whereas the industrialized nations grew at 1.5 percent. Since the trough in 2012, developing countries have grown 5.5 percent versus 0.46 percent in the North.

A significant amount of this growth was due to China's emergence in the world economy and its subsequent demand for developing country goods (especially commodities), and the price effect that comes with such demand. China's growth is at least in part a function of developmental state policies, and other large emerging and developing nations such as India, Brazil and South Africa – all the most significant WTO players – could be called neodevelopmental states as well. We could call this variety "developmental globalization." All of these nations have been slow to open their capital accounts to foreign investment, and maintain capital controls to that end. All engage in industrial and state-led innovation policy to some degree. And together these nations form the heads of significant coalitions in global trade talks that have pushed back on industrialized country proposals aimed at making developing countries look more like industrialized liberal market economies. They have clout because these nations are fast growing markets to which firms and investors want greater access. They have clout because (in purchasing power parity terms) they lead an emerging market world that has a larger share of GDP in the world economy than Western nations. Western nations want that market share.

Development success stories from the twentieth century all struck a unique blend between state and markets not because they just lifted certain policies off the shelf – they did so because they got the *political economy* of industrialization right. Indeed, the risks of trying to deploy capital controls and industrial policy can be at least as concerning as unbridled liberalization. Two key problems can be rent seeking and picking winners (Krueger 1996). The nations with the most success find a way to at least partly circumvent these problems. To circumvent the rent-seeking problem, political scientists have shown that successful industrializers have had states that were "embedded" in the private sector while maintaining "autonomy" from sectional elite interests seeking rents. State agencies that are charged with correcting market failures have to maintain constant communication and input with the private sector (Evans 1995).

Perhaps most importantly, the problem of picking winners has been circumvented by having a good deal of discipline over private actors. Alice Amsden (2001) has referred to the need for "reciprocal control mechanisms." A control mechanism is "a set of institutions that disciplines economic behavior based on a feedback of information that has been sensed and assessed" (2003, 43). In other words, firms have performance requirements that, when they are not met, are no longer supported. The most successful industrializers were able to abandon projects that were not performing; in other countries, such projects were perpetuated because bureaucrats became hijacked by business interests who were dependent on the state.

These two varieties of globalization – a consolidating globalization in the North and a developmental globalization in the South – clash in global trade talks. The theoretical underpinning of the WTO is to aid nations in maximizing their static comparative advantage. This is solidified by the principles of nondiscrimination and national treatment. Nondiscrimination entails treating imports from a nation on the same basis as that given to the most favored other nation. National treatment means that foreign sellers and producers receive the same treatment in a host nation as domestic firms do. Until the last (Uruguay) round of global trade talks, the WTO's predecessor, the General Agreement on Tariffs and Trade (GATT), largely pertained to Western countries and when developing countries took part there were a number of exceptions. All that changed with the establishment of the WTO in 1995, as did the political economy of trade policy.

More than Market Power at the WTO

Developing countries pursuing a more developmental variety of globalization were able to capitalize on their newfound economic power in the Doha Round. In previous trade rounds industrialized nations were able to use their market power to extract concessions by offering market access for regulatory change in the South. In a turnaround, beginning at the turn of the century the developing nations were able to use their market power to exert bargaining power at the WTO. But there was more to it than having a different set of ideas about globalization and development and having newfound economic power. Developing country policies were backed by domestic political actors. Perhaps most importantly, the institutional structure of the WTO worked to their benefit as well.

Many developing countries have sought to globalize in order to achieve a dynamic comparative advantage (Amsden 2001; Wade 2004a). As Amsden suggests, in many cases that entails favoring domestic firms or industries over foreign ones, and thus at least in spirit would violate the principle of national treatment. Tariffs in the world economy are relatively low by historical standards and therefore this clash is often not seen to occur in discussions over goods tariffs. What has gone unrecognized by some is that trade treaties are no longer about trade in goods, but rather are about domestic regulations that could be seen as violating the two principles. Robert Lawrence (1996) has referred to this as "deep" integration, whereas trade talks of yesteryear were "shallow" integration arrangements that just dealt with tariffs and quotas at the economic borders of nations. New rules for services, investment and intellectual property all constrain the ability to maintain financial stability and diversify the product base of a developing economy.

As China, India, Brazil, South Africa and others have continued to grow their economies at a significant pace since the turn of the century, they (and their domestic constituents) have fought hard to maintain at minimum the level of policy space they have at the WTO. Developed nations desperately want market access to these dynamically growing economies, as the industrialized growth is lower and markets have become saturated. At the WTO, this meant rejecting the proposals by the developed world to deepen international investment rules, intellectual property rules, government procurement and financial services (the so-called "Singapore Issues" and others).

Moreover, the developing world turned the tables on the narrative of the talks. Whereas past rounds were pitched to portray the developing world as being riddled with protections that are bad for growth and prosperity, the developing world flipped that on its head and accused the North of the same. Almost immediately in the negotiations the developing world made an issue of industrialized country subsidies and tariffs benefiting agricultural producers, and intellectual property rules that prevented developing countries from breaking patents to serve ailing and diseased populations. In effect, this put the developing world on the moral high ground. Rather than the North getting their Singapore Issues at the 2003 WTO Cancun meetings, the North had to abandon those issues but also amend the WTO agreements on intellectual property rules to allow for public health exceptions – a key victory for developing countries. Turning away from a "deep integration" agenda, from 2003 on, then, the negotiations were mostly about market access in agriculture, manufacturing goods, and some services. In addition, special attention was to go to the poorest nations in the form of relieving cotton subsidies and "aid for trade" packages.

Starting in roughly 2005, the makings of a deal were increased market access and "aid for trade" from the North in exchange for more cuts in

manufacturing and liberalizing financial services in the South. A deal along
those lines was close at the end of 2008: modest cuts in agricultural tariffs and
subsidies by developed countries in return for modest cuts in manufacturing
and services barriers in the developing world.

The problem was that, by all accounts, the gains from trade liberalization
under the round were fairly small. What is more, the losses in terms of trade,
lost policy space and politics were seen as very high. Tariffs were at an all time
low, and the world had already reaped significant gains from previous WTO
rounds of trade liberalization. By the time the Doha Round came around,
there was little left on the table. Chapter 5 goes into this dynamic in great
detail. Under this scenario, global gains projected for 2015 are just $96 billion,
with only $16 billion going to the developing world.

Of the benefits projected for developing countries, only a few see most of
the gains. According to the World Bank, half of all the benefits to developing
countries are expected to flow to just eight countries: Argentina, Brazil (which
stands to receive 23 percent of the developing country benefit), China, India,
Mexico, Thailand, Turkey and Vietnam.

Total tariff losses for developing countries under the "nonagricultural
market access" – or manufactured goods – aspect of the negotiations could be
$63.4 billion, or almost four times the level of benefits. For many developing
countries, slashing tariffs will not only restrict the ability of these countries to
foster new industries so that they may integrate into the world economy, but
it will also limit government funds to support such infant industries and to
maintain social programs for the poor. A majority of developing countries rely
on tariffs for more than one-quarter of their tax revenue. For smaller nations
with little diversification in their economies, tariff revenues provide the core
of government budgets.

In these models, declining terms of trade for developing countries –
the ratio of export to import prices – were also expected to occur in the
developing world. This measure is considered a crucial estimate of the
extent to which a developing country is moving up the value chain in the
global economy, away from primary production and into manufacturing or
knowledge-based economic activities. Since World War I many developing
countries saw their terms of trade deteriorate. Declining terms of trade can
accentuate balance-of-payments problems and make the need to diversify into
other export products ever more urgent (Ocampo and Parra 2003). Under a
likely deal, world prices for agricultural products increase and manufacturing
prices decrease slightly or remain unchanged. According to the Carnegie
Endowment for International Peace, these price changes negatively affect the
terms of trade for developing countries. The report explains that, for many
countries, the rise in world prices for imported food and agricultural goods is

countered with a decline in world prices for their light manufactured exports, such as apparel. This partly explains the welfare losses for Bangladesh, East Africa and the rest of Sub-Saharan Africa.

There was also significant concern about the economic and political cost of lost policy space. As noted earlier, to diversify, developing countries often look at the example of the US and European economies, and more recently, the economies of South Korea and China. These countries diversified away from primary commodities and light manufacturing while slowly opening their economies. They moved into the world marketplace strategically, protecting their major export industries in order to nurture them to compete in world markets. The extent to which the WTO and regional PTAs restrict policy space for industrial diversification is examined later in Chapter 4.

Those small gains to begin with, alongside losses in terms of tariffs, terms of trade and lost policy space, made the Doha Round difficult for developing countries from the start (Gallagher 2008b). Still, a deal was close in 2008 – though it ended up being scuttled by a US refusal to grant poorer nations exceptions to cuts so they can build competitive national industries and protect their economies from unfair or unequal competition. Since 2008 there have been many false starts, but no movement. Despite the mammoth market power of the developed world, developing countries leveraged their newfound economic power to stop proposals they saw as harmful. Developing countries assumed the moral high ground in the talks by pointing to massive agricultural subsidies in the US and Europe and US and EU proposal positions on intellectual property that were threatening the treatment of global health pandemics.

This leveraging on the part of developing countries would not have been able to occur if it was not for the way the WTO is structured. Institutions matter too. The WTO has a one-country/one-vote consensus voting system. Moreover, under a "single undertaking," every country had to agree on every letter of a deal with no individual amendments. Nations like Brazil, India, South Africa and China were all part of key coalitions on agricultural subsidies (G-20), manufacturing (NAMA), food security (G-33) and poverty (G-90). By banding together, they were able to mount a united front against developed country proposals and for their own proposals for market access and policy space.

From an institutional perspective, it was also important that developing countries were preserving existing policy space rather than trying to carve out new space. During its founding by the industrial victors of World War II, and for almost fifty years afterwards, the GATT granted rich and poor countries a lot of flexibility. The GATT and other Bretton Woods institutions were founded on "embedded liberalism" and New Deal politics, and saw linking states and markets as a norm for economic and political stability (Rodrik 2011; Helleiner 1994). Although some of this edifice began to be dismantled (beginning in the late 1980s under the Uruguay Round), a relatively large amount of policy space remained intact – not least because many industrialized nations still want the ability to nurture industry for social gain as well (Block 2008).

Domestic politics within the developing countries also play a role. China, India, Brazil and South Africa all have formidable manufacturing classes, and in the case of India and Brazil, significant financial services and health industries. These interests have pushed their governments to make cuts in those sectors that have been modest at best. Take Brazil, for example. Brazil has a large industrial class and modern financial services, some of which can compete in world markets. In addition, Brazil's soy and beef industries stood to gain significantly from a deal and many manufacturing firms stood to gain in terms of providing machinery, transport and other inputs. Finally – and this is important – the Brazilian real was relatively undervalued during the first years of the Doha Round. A weak currency is implicitly import substituting and a subsidy to exports. Thus, Brazilian industry was more open to negotiating. All this changed after the global financial crisis, as Brazil and many other emerging markets have seen their currencies appreciate by more than 40 percent. Brazilian industrialists are now very averse to a deal because they lack competitiveness and see more concessions as being out of the question.[1]

The Paradoxical Rise of Regionalism

The good news for global trade is that, as the distribution of market power has become more dispersed among income classes at the WTO, the power of liberal and coordinated market economies in the developed world has waned. Thus, the WTO has become *relatively* more equity enhancing than during the Uruguay Round and relative to BITs and PTAs. There is more policy space for a variety of development strategies at the WTO because developing countries now have the power to leverage policy space (and maintain old space). If such strategies truly are more welfare enhancing then an equity-enhanced multilateralism at the WTO will be more optimal.

However, developed nations have become frustrated with their inability to push through a deal at the WTO, and the result is a proliferation of regional and bilateral preferential trade agreements (PTAs). Indeed, shortly after the 2003 Cancun meetings, the United States embarked on a stated policy of "competitive liberalization" whereby the US sought to sign smaller PTAs in order to surround the key nations at the WTO and make them succumb to US proposals (Evenett 2008).

Whether it be capital controls (Chapter 2 of this book), sovereign debt restructuring (Chapter 3), or industrial policy (Chapter 4), the PTAs negotiated by the US and to a lesser (but real) extent by the EU constrain the ability of developing nations to deploy policies for stability and growth in a manner much further than the WTO (Shadlen 2005a; Gallagher 2008a, 2008b; Gallagher and Thrasher 2010). What is paradoxical is that some of those nations are core members of coalitions at the WTO where shallower versions of the same proposals are rejected.

This paradox is looked at head on in Chapter 6. In these cases lies the more traditional story. Most, if not all, of the countries with which the North signs PTAs are miniscule in economic size relative to the North itself. Here, as Hirschman (1945) showed more than a generation ago, is where asymmetric bargaining power and influence can play such a big role – especially when the institutions are asymmetric. The average size of the US economy relative to its negotiating partners is orders-of-magnitude larger. Therefore, in large part the negotiation becomes the classic market-access-for-regulatory-reform equation (Shadlen 2005a, Gallagher 2008b).

Hirschman noted that developing nations will be more apt to succumb to the negotiating positions of industrial countries when the industrialized nation has a large and growing economy relative to the developing nation, and if the developing nation has fewer export options (Hirschman 1945, 18). This is exactly the case in US–Latin American trade relations and goes a long way in explaining why Latin American nations abandon their WTO positions to sign PTAs with the US. Left over from the Cold War, the US has a "generalized system of preferences" (GSP) where developing countries get duty-free access to a number of markets in the US. These have been in place for some time and many nations' export orientation has become geared toward the US. These preferences have to be renewed on a regular basis in the US Congress. As part of the competitive liberalization strategy, the US offered permanent and expanded access that built on the GSP, in exchange for tough rules on intellectual property, investment, services and so forth. Some nations had more than 40 percent of all exports going to the US. It therefore became an offer that couldn't be refused if one wanted to stay in office (Gallagher 2008a). Given that many Latin American nations have fewer opportunities to export those same products to other countries, Hirschman's framework is of particular relevance.

That is not the whole story, however. Domestic politics and collective action also play a role. It was just mentioned that many domestic interests become highly mobilized in support of a PTA with the US because they would be "losers" without a treaty (first surmised by Shadlen 2008). What is more, they will benefit from the reciprocity of a treaty because, being the more globalized sectors, they naturally import more inputs than domestic firms. Put another way, in a developing nation where there are few sectors that are export ready, and those sectors that are export ready stand to lose their market share, the short-term beneficiaries of a "deep" PTA with the US are highly concentrated while the medium- and long-term losers – those who would benefit from a more diversified economy and more widely shared advances in economic welfare – are dispersed.

Unlike the Brazils of the world that already have significant sectors that will lobby for more policy space, many other developing countries, from Nicaragua to Peru, simply do not have a sector that will lobby for policy space that would enable diversification. By the very nature of the economy, a sector that would benefit from economic diversification and industrial policy does not exist and thus cannot have voice in the politics of the negotiation. The same is true for consumers who would benefit in the present or future if a more diversified and stable economy was achieved. According to common understanding of trade policy, static losers are concentrated and static winners are dissipated, and therefore good trade deals may not get through the politics because the losers are more politically organized. The reverse has been true on both sides of the US–Latin America equation. The static winners are very concentrated and the medium- to long-term beneficiaries do not exist or are not competitive enough to exert enough political influence. This has played a key role in some Latin American cases.

Finally, ideology has really mattered in US–Latin American trade relations. The nations that signed deals with the US happened (at the time) to be dominated by right or center-right governments that were ideologically committed to the "Washington Consensus" and were indeed trying to out-liberalize one another. Those nations that are more to the center or center-left such as Brazil, Argentina, Ecuador, Bolivia and Venezuela have refused to negotiate bilaterally with the US at all, and prefer the WTO.

Note

1 As stated by C. Amorim in a personal interview with the author at Harvard University, June 2011.

Chapter 2

LOSING CONTROL: POLICY SPACE TO REGULATE CROSS-BORDER FINANCIAL FLOWS

This chapter examines the extent to which measures to mitigate the current crisis and prevent future crises are permissible under a variety of bilateral, regional and multilateral trade and investment agreements. The principal tool that is analyzed are regulations of cross-border finance, a measure traditionally referred to as "capital controls." Such measures have been important parts of the development toolkit as they can play a role in preventing and mitigating financial crises, to manage exchange rates and to steer credit toward productive development. This chapter shows that the ability to deploy such regulations is fairly constrained under the WTO, but even more so under US trade and investment agreements.

Introduction

Since the Great Depression, and very much so in the run-up to and in the wake of the current financial crisis, some nations have relied on capital controls as one of many possible tools to mitigate or prevent the financial instability that can come with short-term inflows and outflows of capital. In the bubble years before the 2008 global financial crisis became acute, nations such as China, Colombia, India and Thailand regulated inflows of capital in order to stem those bubbles. When the crisis hit, nations like Iceland, Indonesia, Russia, Argentina and Ukraine put capital controls on outflows of capital to "stop the bleeding" related to the crisis (International Monetary Fund 2009).

As I show in this chapter, the economic evidence is fairly strong for the use of capital controls. However, there is concern that the myriad trade and investment treaties across the world may prohibit the use of measures to prevent and mitigate financial bubbles and subsequent crises. There are a number of works that examine the policy space for industrial development, but very few that examine policy space for measures pertaining to financial stability

(Shadlen 2005a; Gallagher 2005; Anderson 2009; Mayer 2009). This chapter conducts a comparative analysis to pinpoint the extent to which nations have the policy space for capital controls in the world economy.

The major findings of this research are exhibited in Table 2.1, where policy space under the WTO, US bilateral investment treaties (BITs) and free trade agreements (FTAs), and other BITs and FTAs by other capital-exporting countries is presented. Under no regime are capital controls permitted for current transactions unless sanctioned by the IMF. For the capital account however, there is interesting variation.

The WTO allows for nations to deploy capital controls on both inflows and outflows as long as nations have not committed to the liberalization of certain financial services. If a nation has made commitments in financial services, restrictions on inflows are not permitted. However, it will be shown that there are safeguard measures that may apply. In terms of recourse, if a nation that has liberalized financial services does restrict capital inflows or outflows, that

Table 2.1. Policy space for capital controls: A comparison

	IMF	OECD	WTO	US BITS/ FTAs
Permissible capital controls				
Current	No	No	No	**No**
Capital				
inflows	Yes	No	No*	**No**
outflows	Yes	No	No*	**No**
Safeguard provisions				
Current	Yes**	Yes**	Yes**	**No**
Capital				
inflows	N/A	Yes	No	**No**
outflows	N/A	Yes	Yes	**No**
Number of countries covered	186	30	69	58
Dispute resolution format	Member vote	Member vote	State-to-state	Investor-state
Enforcement instrument	Loss of membership	Loss of membership	Retaliation	Investor compensation

* Capital controls fully permissible for nations that have not committed to liberalize cross-border trade in financial services.
** Permitted only under IMF approval.

nation could be subject to a dispute panel that could rule that the nation deploying the measure could be retaliated against.

US BITs and FTAs do not permit restrictions on inflows or outflows. If a nation does restrict either type of capital flow they can be subject to investor-state arbitration whereby the government of the host state would pay for the "damages" accrued to the foreign investor. The BITs and FTAs of other major capital exporters, such as those negotiated by the EU, Japan, China and Canada, either completely "carve out" host country legislation on capital controls (therefore permitting them) or allow for a temporary safeguard on inflows and outflows to prevent or mitigate a financial crisis. The US does not have either measure. However, a handful of FTAs have recently allowed for a grace period whereby foreign investors are not allowed to file claims against a host state until after the crisis period has subsided.

Following this brief introduction, the chapter is divided into four additional parts. The second part of the chapter provides a brief overview of the economic theory, policy and evidence regarding capital controls. The third part of the chapter examines policy space for capital controls under the WTO. Part four of the chapter conducts a comparative analysis that juxtaposes US treaties alongside the WTO and the regional and bilateral treaties of other major capital-exporting countries. Part five of the chapter summarizes the key findings and offers policy recommendations.

Capital Account Liberalization and Capital Controls: Theory and Evidence

Advocates for capital market liberalization argue that, by liberalizing the flows of international capital, developing countries would benefit by getting access to cheaper credit and investment from developed markets, promoting growth and stability. Indeed, conventional theory implies that investment tends to flow to developing countries, where the marginal returns may be higher (Barro 1997). That view, based on the assumption of perfect capital markets, has been largely discredited with the recent experiences of currency crises (Ocampo et al. 2008). International capital flows tend to be procyclical, creating excess inflows during booms and causing capital flight in moments of instability, further aggravating crises.

Moreover, it has been shown that capital market liberalization in developing countries is not associated with economic growth (Prasad et al. 2003). Indeed, the most recent research has shown that capital market liberalization is only associated with growth in nations that have reached a certain institutional threshold – a threshold that most developing nations are yet to achieve (Kose et al. 2009). This is partly due to the fact that the binding constraint for some developing country growth trajectories is not the need for external investment, but the lack of investment demand. This constraint can be accentuated through foreign capital flows because such flows appreciate the real exchange rate, thus reducing the competitiveness of goods and reducing private sector willingness to invest (Rodrik and Subramanian 2009).

Capital controls have been found to stabilize short-term volatile capital flows; and can give policymakers additional policy instruments that allow them more effective and less costly macroeconomic stabilization measures; can promote growth and increase economic efficiency by reducing the volatility of financing and of real macroeconomic performance; and can discourage long-term capital outflows (IMF 2010). The literature on capital controls generally discusses at least six (somewhat overlapping) core reasons why nations may want to deploy them (Magud and Reinhart 2006). These can be referred to as "the six fears" of capital flows:

1. **Fear of appreciation**: capital inflows cause upward pressure on the value of the domestic currency, making domestic producers less competitive in the international market, hurting exports and therefore the economy.
2. **Fear of "hot money"**: the large injection of money into a small economy may cause distortions, and eventually a sudden reversion if foreign investors try to leave simultaneously.
3. **Fear of large inflows**: large volumes of capital inflows, even if not all hot money, can cause dislocations in the financial system.
4. **Fear of loss of monetary autonomy**: a trinity is always at work: it is not possible to have a fixed (or highly managed) exchange rate, monetary policy autonomy and open capital markets. Specifically, when central banks intervene in the exchange market buying foreign currency in order to curb the appreciation of the exchange rate, they effectively increase the domestic monetary base. Trying to raise interest rates to offset that effect causes more capital inflows, as foreign investors rush in to take advantage of higher yields.
5. **Fear of asset bubbles**, raised by Ocampo and Palma (2008): This is a particularly important issue in the 2008 financial crisis, since the bursting of the real estate bubble was the root cause of the banking crisis around the globe.
6. **Fear of capital "flight"**: capital may rapidly leave a nation in the event of a crisis or because of contagion (Grabel 2003; Epstein 2005).

Table 2.2 exhibits a sample of various types of capital controls that have been deployed by nations to address these fears.

Table 2.2. Capital controls and capital management techniques

Inflows
Restrictions on currency mismatches*
End use limitations**
Unremunerated reserve requirements***
Taxes on inflows
Minimum stay requirements
Limits on domestic firms and residents from borrowing in foreign currencies
Mandatory approvals for capital transactions
Prohibitions on inflows
Outflows
Limits on ability of foreigners to borrow domestically
Exchange controls
Taxes/restrictions on outflows
Mandatory approvals for capital transactions
Prohibitions on outflows

* Borrowing abroad only allowed for investment and foreign trade.
** Only companies with foreign currency reserves can borrow abroad.
*** Percent of short-term inflows kept in deposit in local currency for specified time.
Sources: Ocampo, Kregel and Griffith-Jones (2007), Epstein, Grabel and Jomo (2008).

Economists usually differentiate between capital controls on capital inflows and controls on outflows. Moreover, measures are usually categorized as being "price-based" or "quantity-based" controls. Table 2.2 lists examples of controls on inflows and outflows, though sometimes the distinction can be murky (Epstein et al. 2008; Ocampo et al. 2007). Examples of quantity-based controls are restrictions on currency mismatches, and minimum-stay requirements and end-use limitations. Many of these have been used by nations such as China and India. Examples of price-based controls include taxes on inflows (Brazil) or on outflows (Malaysia). Unremunerated reserve requirements (URR) are both. On one hand they are price-based restrictions on inflows, but they also include a minimum-stay requirement which can act like a quantity-based restriction on outflows.

Controls are most often targeting foreign currency and local currency debt of a short-term nature. Foreign direct investment (except for FDI in the financial sector) is often considered less volatile and worrisome from the standpoint of macroeconomic stability. Inflow restrictions on currency debt can reduce the overall level of such borrowing and steer investment toward longer-term productive investments and thus reduce risk. Taxes on such investment cut the price differential between short- and long-term debt and thus discourage investment in shorter-term obligations. Outflows restrictions and measures are usually deployed to "stop the bleeding" and keep capital from leaving the host nation too rapidly.

The literature on the effectiveness of capital controls is too vast to cover here. However, two comprehensive assessments of the literature have recently been conducted. In sum, the literature strongly supports the use of capital controls on inflows. Evidence on outflows is more controversial. Magud and Reinhart (2006) conducted the most accurate assessment of the literature to 2006. In their analysis, they expressed concern over the lack of a unified theoretical framework to analyze the macroeconomic consequences of the controls, the heterogeneity of countries and control measures, the multiplicity of policy goals and what constitutes "success." As most studies investigate a few country cases (mainly Chile and Malaysia), it is difficult to make generalized conclusions from the literature in the field. Theirs is the most valiant attempt to overcome these shortcomings. What's more, the authors also "weight" the findings in the literature with respect to their econometric rigor.

To summarize, say Magud and Reinhart, "in sum, capital controls on inflows seem to make monetary policy more independent, alter the composition of capital flows and reduce real exchange rate pressures" (2006, 365). In terms of outflows, it is clear that such provisions were successful in Malaysia, but it is not so clear about the case of other nations.

In a February 2010 Staff Position Note, the IMF staff reviewed all the evidence on capital controls on inflows, pre- and post-crisis, and concluded: "capital controls – in addition to both prudential and macroeconomic policy – are justified as part of the policy toolkit to manage inflows. Such controls, moreover, can retain potency even if investors devise strategies to bypass them, provided such strategies are more costly than the expected return from the transaction: the cost of circumvention strategies acts as 'sand in the wheels'" (IMF 2010, 5). To come to this conclusion, this recent and landmark IMF study reviews the experiences of post–Asian crisis capital controls. The IMF also conducted its own cross-country analysis in this study, which produced profound findings. The econometric analysis conducted by the IMF examined how countries that used capital controls fared versus countries that did not use them in the run-up to the current crisis. They found that countries with controls fared better: "the use of capital controls was associated with avoiding some of the worst growth outcomes associated with financial fragility" (IMF 2010, 19).

There has even been some attention by prominent economists on the need for restrictions on outflows. Calvo (2009) argues that capital controls could be deployed to dampen the impact of capital flight during crises. Even in "normal" times, however, Calvo argues that prudential regulations should sometimes be coupled with foreign exchange restrictions to reduce capital flight.

To summarize, there is an emerging consensus in the economics profession regarding capital controls. Capital controls, especially those on inflows, are increasingly seen as a prudential measure for developing countries hoping to prevent and mitigate financial crises.

Policy Space for Capital Controls at the WTO

This section of the chapter examines the extent to which the WTO grants nations the policy space to deploy capital controls. The key piece of WTO law that covers capital flows is the General Agreement on Trade in Services (GATS). The GATS is currently the only binding multilateral pact that disciplines capital controls, though specific countries may have certain freedoms if the governments in place in the 1990s did not make widespread commitments in the financial services sector. More specifically:

- A member is most protected from a WTO challenge over capital controls if it committed no financial services sectors to GATS coverage in any mode.
- However, even nations that have made widespread commitments in financial services may have – if challenged – recourse to various exceptions, although these have not been tested and the record of WTO exceptions in other contexts is not reassuring.
- The policy space for controls on *current* account transactions defers to the IMF.

GATS

The GATS is part of the Marrakesh Treaty that serves as an umbrella for the various agreements reached at the end of the Uruguay Round of GATT negotiations that established the WTO. The GATS provides a general framework disciplining policies "affecting trade in services" and establishes a commitment for periodic future negotiations. On the one hand, the GATS is divided into a part on "General Obligations," which binds all members. These include the obligation to provide most favored nation treatment to all WTO members (Article II) and some disciplines on nondiscriminatory domestic regulations that are still being fully developed (Article VI).

On the other hand, the GATS also includes a part dealing with "Specific Commitments," which apply only to the extent that countries choose to adopt them by listing them in their country specific schedules. These cover primarily the disciplines of Market Access (Article XVI) and National Treatment (Article XVII) (Raghavan 2009).

Numerous annexes cover rules for specific sectors: the Annexes on Financial Services are of particular relevance for capital controls. However, trade in services occurs across the four services modes discussed in the GATS in general:

Mode 1: *Cross-border supply* is defined to cover services flows from the territory of one member into the territory of another member (for example banking or architectural services transmitted via telecommunications or mail);

Mode 2: *Consumption abroad* happens when the consumer travels outside of the country to access a service such as tourism, education, health care and so forth;

Mode 3: *Commercial presence* occurs when the user of a financial service is immobile and the provider is mobile, implying that the financial service supplier of one WTO member establishes a territorial presence, possibly through ownership or lease, in another member's territory to provide a financial service (for example subsidiaries of foreign banks in a domestic territory); and

Mode 4: *Presence of natural persons* occurs when financial services are supplied by individuals of one country in the territory of another.

IMF analysts have found that about 16 countries have significant Mode 1 commitments in financial services, while around 50 each have significant Mode 2 and 3 commitments for the sector – this includes most OECD countries (Valckx 2002; Kireyev 2002).

Generally speaking, GATS negotiations and commitments are of a "positive list" approach, whereby nations only commit to bind specified sectors to GATS disciplines. This stands in contrast with a "negative list approach," which is more common for goods negotiations and in most FTAs. In a negative list or "top-down" approach, negotiators assume that all sectors will be covered in some way, except a handful that are listed by particular nations.

WTO members have recourse to binding dispute-settlement procedures, where perceived violations of GATS commitments can be challenged and retaliatory sanctions or payments authorized as compensation.

Capital account liberalization, capital controls and GATS

Unbeknownst to many, GATS commitments require the simultaneous opening of the capital account. Those nations that make commitments under Modes 1 and 3 for financial services are required to permit capital to flow freely to the extent that such capital is an integral part of the service provided – though some exceptions may apply. GATS Article XVI on Market Access contains a footnote (8) that references capital liberalization:

> If a Member undertakes a market-access commitment in relation to the supply of a service through the mode of supply referred to in subparagraph 2(a) of Article I [i.e. Mode 1] and if the cross-border movement of capital is an essential part of the service itself, *that Member is thereby committed to allow such movement of capital.* If a Member undertakes a market-access commitment in relation to the supply of a service through the mode of supply referred to in subparagraph 2(c) of Article I [i.e. Mode 3], *it is thereby committed to allow related transfers of capital into its territory.* [Italics added]

While Modes 1 and 3 are explicitly referred to here, Article XI (2) also refers to capital liberalization:

> Nothing in this Agreement shall affect the rights and obligations of the members of the International Monetary Fund under the Articles of Agreement of the Fund, including the use of exchange actions which are in conformity with the Articles of Agreement, provided that a Member shall not impose restrictions on any capital transactions inconsistently with its specific commitments regarding such transactions, except under Article XII or at the request of the Fund.

Taken together, these provisions indicate that a country that makes GATS financial service commitments in the modes of cross-border trade (Mode 1) and establishment of commercial presence (Mode 3) may explicitly be required to open its capital account. In such instances, the nation's ability to deploy capital controls *related to capital inflows* would be restricted. The text is silent on whether capital controls related to capital outflows are similarly disciplined.

As an aside, capital account transactions are not restricted under the IMF Articles of Agreement, and thus nations are free to choose whether capital controls are part of their arsenal to prevent and mitigate financial crises. However, a distinction needs to be made with respect to *financial services* and *capital flows.* Under the GATS, nations liberalize specific types of financial services, such as banking, securities, insurance and so forth – which does not necessarily imply capital movements or changes in fundamental capital account regulation.

However, there are scenarios where the liberalization of financial services will require an open capital account. The IMF cites the following Mode 1 example, where "a loan extended by a domestic bank to a foreign customer using internationally raised capital creates international capital flows and international trade in financial services. To the extent that a financial services transaction involved an international capital transaction, the capital account needs to be opened for the former to take place freely" (Kireyev 2002). Another paper by an IMF official provides examples of how the GATS Mode 1 essentially requires the liberalization of a capital account:

> To the extent that a member restricts its residents from borrowing from non-residents, a member's commitment to allow banks of other members to provide cross-border lending services to its nationals would require a relaxation of this restriction. Similarly, if a member also makes a commitment to permit non-resident banks to provide cross-border deposit services, such a commitment would require the member to liberalize restrictions it may have imposed on the ability of residents to hold accounts abroad. In these respects, the GATS serves to liberalize the making of both inward and outward investments. (Hagan 2000, 24)

This is echoed in a recent book by Sydney Key, who says: "The bottom line is that if a country makes a commitment to liberalize trade with respect to a particular financial service in the GATS, it is also making a commitment to liberalize most capital movements associated with the trade liberalization commitment" (2003, 20). The WTO, in a recent paper (2010a), quoted from Key's work to make the same point. In other words, liberalizing cross-border trade in financial services (Mode 1) may need an open capital account to facilitate such trade, which of course results in international capital flows. A similar scenario can be outlined in terms of Mode 3 liberalization. A loan extended by a foreign bank to a domestic client requiring capital to be transferred from the parent company of the foreign bank to its subsidiary abroad would also require an open capital account. In any event, it is worth noting that WTO panels are not bound to the IMF's distinction between service transactions and capital flows.

If a nation has not listed cross-border trade in financial services (Mode 1) or commercial presence of foreign services (Mode 3), that country may be free to deploy capital controls as they see fit. Indeed, numerous developing nations have not "listed" the liberalization of cross-border trade in financial services nor Mode 3 commitments under the GATS. According to the WTO, the majority of developing countries made relatively fewer commitments in financial services related to capital markets (WTO 2010a).

It is also possible that certain types of measures may be more GATS compliant than others. Article XVI, paragraph 2 is seen as a nonexhaustive list of the types of financial services whereby a host nation "shall not maintain" restrictions on the flow of capital. The list of measures does not explicitly mention any of the capital controls and other capital management techniques found in Table 2.2 of this report. Therefore a case could be made that capital controls of the kind discussed in Table 2.2 of this report are not even covered by the GATS.

If a nation's capital controls were found in violation of its GATS commitments, it could invoke one or more exceptions in the GATS text. A first option would be to claim that the measure was taken for prudential reasons under Article 2(a) of the Annex on Financial Services. This exception reads:

> Notwithstanding any other provisions of the Agreement, a Member shall not be prevented from taking measures for prudential reasons, including for the protection of investors, depositors, policy holders or persons to whom a fiduciary duty is owed by a financial service supplier, or to ensure the integrity and stability of the financial system. Where such measures do not conform with the provisions of the Agreement, they shall not be used as a means of avoiding the Member's commitments or obligations under the Agreement.

Inflows controls such as unremunerated reserve requirements or inflows taxes could be argued to be of a prudential nature, especially given the new IMF report discussed earlier. However, the sentence stating that prudential measures "shall not be used as a means of avoiding the member's commitments or obligations under the Agreement" is regarded by some as self-cancelling and thus of limited utility (Tucker and Wallach 2009; Raghavan 2009). Others, however, do not see the measure to be second guessing but rather "as a means of catching hidden opportunistic and protectionist measures masquerading as prudential" (Van Aaken and Kurtz 2009, 18). Still others point out that, in contrast with other parts of the GATS that require a host nation to defend the "necessity" of the measure, there is no necessity test for the prudential exception in the GATS. This arguably gives nations more room to deploy controls. Indeed, Argentina lost cases related to controls under BITs because they failed such a "necessity test" (Burke-White 2008). Nations have requested that the WTO elaborate on what is and is not covered in the prudential exception, but such requests have fallen on deaf ears (Cornford 2004). And as of this writing, the prudential exception has not been tested.

If a country's capital controls were found in violation of its GATS commitments in financial services, it could also invoke Article XII, Restrictions to Safeguard the Balance of Payments. Paragraph 1 of Article XII states:

> In the event of serious balance-of-payments and external financial difficulties or threat thereof, a Member may adopt or maintain restrictions on trade in services on which it has undertaken specific commitments, including on payments or transfers for transactions related to such commitments. It is recognized that particular pressures on the balance of payments of a Member in the process of economic development or economic transition may necessitate the use of restrictions to ensure, inter alia, the maintenance of a level of financial reserves adequate for the implementation of its programme of economic development or economic transition.

The next paragraph specifies that such measures can be deployed as long as they do not discriminate among other WTO members, are consistent with the IMF articles (thus pertain only to capital account controls), "avoid unnecessary damage" to other members, do "not exceed those necessary" to deal with the balance-of-payments problem, and are temporary and phased out progressively.

It may be extremely difficult for a capital control to meet all of these conditions, especially the hurdles dealing with the notion of "necessity," a slippery concept in trade law that countries have had difficulty proving. Moreover, concern has been expressed about the extent to which the balance-of-payments exception provides nations with the policy place for restrictions on capital inflows that are more preventative in nature and may occur before "serious" balance-of-payments difficulties exist (Hagan 2000). If a nation does choose to use this derogation, the nation is required to notify the WTO's Balance of Payments Committee (described below).

Table 2.3 lists the 36 nations that have committed to scheduling the liberalization of some combination of Modes 1, 2 and 3 under the GATS (Valckx 2002). These nations would be the most prone to being disciplined under GATS. Finally, there is not a reassuring record of countries being able to invoke exceptions at the WTO.

Capital controls and current transactions

Capital controls on the inflows or outflows of dividends, interest payments and the like are *current account* restrictions. Remember that, as a rule, the IMF Articles of Agreement do not permit current account restrictions. However, the

Table 2.3. Most vulnerable to actions against capital controls under GATS

Argentina	Japan	Panama
Australia	Kuwait	Philippines
Bahrain	Kyrgyz Republic	Qatar
Canada	Latvia	Romania
Ecuador	Macau	Sierra Leone
Estonia	Malawi	Singapore
Gabon	Mauritius	Solomon Islands
Gambia	Mongolia	South Africa
Hong Kong	Mozambique	Switzerland
Hungary	New Zealand	Tunisia
Iceland	Nigeria	Turkey
Indonesia	Norway	United Arab Emirates
		USA

Source: Valckx (2002).

IMF may recommend diversion from those rules during a crisis and/or under an IMF financial program. In these circumstances, Article XI, paragraph 2 of the GATS applies. This article states that the IMF has jurisdiction over these types of circumstances and the GATS does not apply. Therefore, when a country is permitted by the IMF as part of an IMF financial program to pursue capital controls on current transactions, as has been the case with Iceland in 2008–2009, then the WTO has no jurisdiction over the use of controls.

When a nation seeks to pursue capital controls related to the current account and such actions are not part of an IMF Financial program, the nation has the potential to do so but has to submit a request to the WTO's Balance of Payments Committee.

The Balance of Payments Committee

Any capital control involving capital or current account restrictions must be submitted to the Committee on Balance-of-Payments Restrictions, which was established for the earlier BOP safeguard under GATT and was traditionally responsible for consultation dealing with trade restriction for balance-of-payment purposes. The same body and procedures now apply to financial and other services.

The committee has never pronounced on any current or capital account restrictions related to financial services, but the GATS text specifies that consultations related to these matters can evaluate whether the CMT meets the various criteria outlined above, whether "alternative corrective measures [...] may be available," and "in particular" whether the measure is progressively phased out (GATS 1994).

This is a unique procedure in the GATS. While the WTO compatibility of a country's domestic policy normally is only tested through formal dispute-settlement proceedings, CMTs face an additional set of hurdles and proceedings under Article XII.

Returning to some of the key questions outlined above, the following can be said about the WTO in relation to capital controls. While the WTO's financial services provisions remain untested in formal dispute settlement, they nonetheless represent the world's only multilateral body with enforcement capacity to discipline capital controls, on terms that provide less policy space than the IMF Articles of Agreement. Capital controls may be disciplined under the WTO for approximately fifty of the WTO members. If a nation has made commitments in financial services, restrictions on inflows are explicitly mentioned in the market access provisions of the GATS (though not one capital control is explicitly listed in the nonexhaustive list) but outflows may also be covered. In terms of compliance, the potential penalty for noncompliance is sustained cash payments or cross-retaliation rights to a large set of complaining countries. When nations file claims, the dispute resolution process is "state-to-state" rather than "investor-state" which will be discussed later in the report.

Capital Controls in US Trade and Investment Treaties

The US has engaged in investment-treaty making since its War of Independence through what were called Friendship, Commerce and Navigation Treaties. The successors to those agreements are bilateral investment treaties (BITs), which the US has been negotiating since 1977. The US did not invent BITs; Europeans have BITs going back to 1959. Indeed, there are now close to two thousand BITs in existence. Beginning with NAFTA in 1994, US FTAs also have investment provisions analogous to those found in BITs. Finally BITs and FTAs also include provisions on financial services.

The US has concluded 46 BITs since 1977, and more recently has used very similar language to the BITs as part of investment chapters in 12 US free trade agreements (FTAs) (Vandevelde 2008). This section of the chapter reveals that US-style investment rules run far deeper and include many more limitations on the ability of nations to deploy capital controls. Specifically, US investment rules:

- Elevate the rights of US capital investors over domestic capital investors, whereby US investors can file claims against violating parties through an investor-state dispute-settlement process and receive financial compensation for violations, while domestic investors do not have such rights;
- Do not permit restrictions on both capital inflows and outflows;
- Provide no clear exceptions for balance-of-payments exceptions, though some FTAs provide a grace period for filing investor-state claims.

This section of the chapter will have two parts. The first part will be a short background on the purpose and main provisions of US BITs and investment components of FTAs. The second part will be an examination of the extent to which nations may deploy capital controls under US BITs and FTAs.

Investment provisions in US BITs and FTAs

BITs and investment provisions in US FTAs have evolved over time to have at least five general features. Normally, through an inter-agency process and with input from outside experts and interests, the US puts together a "Model BIT" that serves as the template for negotiations for BITs and FTAs:

> The model would be tendered to the other party at the beginning of negotiations with the hope that agreement would be reached on a text that did not differ substantively or even in a significant stylistic way from the model. If too many departures from the model were demanded by the other party, then no BIT would be concluded. (Vandevelde 2008, 1)

Scholars have characterized the model BITs and subsequent treaties as occurring in three "waves;" from 1981 to early 1989 where 35 BITs were negotiated, from the early 1990s to 2002 where the NAFTA and a handful of BITs were signed, and from 2002 to the present where FTAs with Chile, Singapore and Central America were negotiated (Vandevelde 2008). In 2009 the US engaged in a review of the 2004 Model BIT that formed the core of most US BITs and investment components of FTAs. The new model was released in 2012 and may be used for negotiations of BITs with China, India and Brazil, and in FTAs negotiations with Pacific nations.

This chapter will focus on the treaties completed up through the 2004 model BIT, the last being the BIT with Rwanda and the FTAs with Peru, Colombia, Panama and South Korea. In terms of coverage, whereas the earliest BITs and FTAs focused almost solely on foreign direct investment, contemporary treaties cover both inflows and outflows of virtually all types of investment, including equities, securities, loans, derivatives, sovereign debt and the financial services facilitators of such flows. According to Vandevelde (2008), there are five general components of US BITs and subsequent provisions in US FTAs:

1. **Minimum Standard of Treatment** that an investor should enjoy, including national treatment and most favored nation-states in both the pre-establishment and post-establishment rights. On an absolute level, US investors are to receive "fair and equitable treatment and full protection in accordance to customary international law" (United States of America 2004).
2. **Restrictions on Expropriation**. BITs and FTAs strictly forbid the direct or indirect expropriation of US investments absent prompt and full compensation.
3. **Free Transfers**. US nationals and firms must be permitted to freely transfer payments in and out of a host country "without delay." This will be discussed in detail below.
4. **No Performance Requirements**. US BITs forbid nations from imposing performance requirements such as local content rules, joint venture and research and development requirements, export requirements, rules related to personnel decisions and so forth.
5. **Investor-State Arbitration**. In stark contrast to dispute settlement under the WTO and all other aspects of FTAs other than investment rules, US firms have the right to binding arbitration of disputes related to violations of the agreements. As is the case with most BITs across the world, foreign firms do not have to file claims through governments but can take a claim to an arbitral panel, often the International Centre for the Settlement of Investment Disputes (ICSID) at the World Bank for any perceived violation of the above principles.

In addition to these core elements, US treaties often have some so-called "exceptions" such as for essential security, matters related to taxation (where there is another body of US international law) and others. Finally, post-2004 BITs have putative limitations on the ability of host states to reduce environment or labor laws to attract foreign investment. Before moving forward, it should be underscored that these treaties elevate foreign investor rights over domestic investors, as they do not require the host country's firms to liberalize their investments, nor do they permit host country investors to use investor-state arbitration (Hagan 2000).

Capital controls and US BITs and FTAs

The free transfer of funds to and from the US is a core principle of US BITs and FTAs, as well as those of most other capital-exporting countries. When a host nation violates that principle, or if capital transfers violate the other principles, a nation could be subject to an investor-state arbitration claim where they could be sued for damages. All of the US BITs and FTAs therefore restrict the ability of host nations to deploy capital controls (Anderson 2009a). Argentina, after its crisis in 2001–2002 was subject to numerous such claims in the hundreds of millions of dollars.

All US BITs and FTAs require host nations to permit free transfers without delay of all types of covered investments. Moreover, financial services are covered in BITs and comprise a separate chapter in FTAs. Analogous to the GATS, if a nation commits to liberalizing financial services, the free flow of such investment are covered there as well. It should be noted, however, that under the services chapters of FTAs, dispute resolution is state-to-state.

Over the years US treaties have listed numerous types of investments covered, such as securities, loans, FDI, bonds (both sovereign and private) and derivatives. Treaties also make a point to say such a list is nonexhaustive. Taken together, the transfers provisions, along with the other principles of the agreements ensure that an investment can enter and leave a nation freely. If such an investment is restricted, a host nation can be subject to arbitration.

Of all the treaties the US has signed there is only one clear exception to this rule, the balance-of-payments exception found in NAFTA. Article 2014(1) can be invoked when the host state experiences "serious balance of payments difficulties, or the threat thereof." Like similar exceptions at the WTO and OECD, use of the exception must be temporary, nondiscriminatory and be consistent with the IMF Articles of Agreement (thus capital controls can only be aimed at capital account transactions unless approved by the IMF).

"Cooling off" provisions

As discussed earlier, Chile is a nation that has deployed capital controls to some success. The US negotiated FTAs with Chile and Singapore (which had also used capital controls in the wake of the 1997 Asian crisis) at the turn of the century, both came into force in 2004. The limits in the US model on capital controls became major sticking points for both Chile and Singapore. In fact, during the negotiations with Chile, United States Trade Representative (USTR) head Robert Zoellick had to intervene with the finance minister of Chile to salvage the negotiations over this issue. During those negotiations the US negotiated a "compromise" that, with some variation, has been used in agreements with Singapore, Peru and

Colombia. Interestingly, however, it has not become a matter of practice. Such a cooling off period was not included in the 2004 Model BIT nor the FTAs with DR–CAFTA, Panama and others.

The compromise has since become known as the "cooling off" provision whereby the US cannot file a claim for a violation of the investment provisions until a period of one year after the provision has been deployed. The cooling off periods are illustrated in an annex to the agreements. The rationale would be that the host nation may need to address or stem a financial crisis and that the nation should not be subject to claims in the middle of such action. However, and this is important, the cooling off period allows a foreign investor to sue for damages related to capital controls that were deployed during the cooling off year, but cannot file the claim until after that year. To be clear, an investor has to wait one year to file a claim related to capital controls to prevent and mitigate crises, but that claim can be for a measure taken during the cooling off year (Hornbeck 2003).

It should also be noted that these provisions are not mutual. The cooling off period is only for investors suing a party that is not the US. However, there are limits on the absolute amount of damage that an investor can recoup. Loss of profits, loss of business and other similar consequential or incidental damages cannot be recovered. All of these agreements include some exceptions to the annex, instances where the cooling off period and limitation on damages does not apply: payments on current transactions, on transfers associated with equity investments and loan or bond payments.

The cooling off language triggered controversy in the US, leading to hearings specifically on the subject on 1 April 2003 at the Subcommittee on Domestic and International Monetary, Trade and Technology of the Committee on Financial Services in the US House of Representatives (US House of Representatives 2003). The committee was chaired by Congressman Michael Oxley (R-Indiana, majority), with the minority head being Barney Frank (D-Massachusetts, minority). In general, the hearings revealed that most Republicans were against the use of capital controls, whereas Democrats favored more flexibility. The hearings were very lively.

The leading advocate for restricting capital controls was John Taylor, then undersecretary of the US Treasury for International Affairs in the Bush administration. As a Stanford University economist he had become famous for the "Taylor Rule" that sets a formula for inflation targeting. Insiders thus began referring to the cooling off provisions as the "Taylor Provisions." Interestingly, the hearings included harsh rebuttals to Taylor by Nancy Birdsall of the Center for Global Development, Jagdish Bhagwati of Columbia University and Daniel Tarullo, then of Georgetown University and now on the board of governors of the US Federal Reserve System. These individuals are staunch supporters of free trade in goods, but argued that capital account liberalization without exception is dangerous from economic and foreign policy perspectives. Congresswoman Carolyn Maloney (D-New York, now chair of the Joint Economic Committee) argued in favor of flexibility. At the hearings, Barney Frank famously remarked that "ice is in the eyes of the beholder," arguing that the cooling off period still effectively restricts Chile and Singapore from using capital controls (US House of Representatives 2003).

Around the same time senior IMF officials in the legal department wrote articles arguing that BITs should have at least temporary derogations for balance-of-payments difficulties and that the cooling off period was not sufficient. Hagan (2000) expressed concern that if one nation forbids a host country from using capital controls on a temporary basis but the host country is permitted to use controls under agreements with other nations, then the controls will be discriminatory in nature and lead to distortions. Siegel (2004), who called the cooling off provisions "draconian," expressed concern that the US transfers provisions raised jurisdictional issues with the IMF. The US provisions call for free transfers of all current transactions but unlike WTO, OECD and other capital exporters, the US provisions do not include mention of the ability of the IMF to recommend capital controls as part of a financial program. Siegel argues that FTAs "create a risk that in complying with its obligations under the FTA, a member could be rendered ineligible to use the Fund's resources under the Fund's articles" (Siegel 2004, 4). Finally, in meetings with IMF officials concern was expressed over the lack of consistency between US agreements and others. For instance, South Korea has a broad exception under the OECD codes and its other BITs, but not with the US. Which measure holds?

Illustrative discussion of capital controls and violations of US investment rules

It should be clear from the above discussion that capital controls are in fundamental violation of the core principle in US trade and investment treaties that requires the free transfer of funds without delay. That said, it is important to understand exactly how these provisions work in relation to various types of controls. Such an exercise reveals that it is possible that some kinds of capital controls may be able to slip through US investment rules. However, given that there are no derogations in US treaties such possibilities are far from certain.

Capital inflow restrictions such as URRs, minimum-stay requirements and outright prohibitions on certain types of inflows are designed to keep out or slow the flow of short-term inflows into an economy. On the surface, restrictions on inflows may escape violation because an investor has to show that the investor has been "damaged" or that the value of an investment has been diminished in order to file a claim. Instruments to prevent an investment before it occurs therefore may have more "cover" under the agreements. However, restrictions on inflows violate the ability of investors to have market access and national treatment pre-establishment. A claim could arise simply on those grounds, or because an investor that may have made regular previous investments in a host country and suddenly cannot could claim that the investor no longer enjoys fair and equitable treatment and the minimum standard of treatment under the agreement. What's more, if an investor wanted to pull funds from a country that were held by a URR or minimum-stay requirement (as a form of outflow then), the capital control would restrict the free transfer out of the country and clearly be subject to a claim – as would almost all the other outflows measures listed in Table 2.2. Indeed, not only are restrictions on outflows violations of transfers provisions, they can also be seen as expropriations. Moreover, if a nation has committed to liberalizing financial services under the services chapter of an FTA all inflows and outflows that pertain to the (negatively) listed service could not be restricted.

One other possible avenue for policy space may be available for limits by domestic firms or domestic residents in borrowing or lending abroad. Remember that investment rules do not cover domestic investors, nor are domestic investors able to resort to investor-state dispute settlement. On the surface, such a provision would not be subject to a claim as a violation of the transfers provisions because such restrictions to not consider a covered investment. However, it may be possible that a claim could arise by an investor arguing that national treatment principles had been violated. By restricting US banks from lending in dollars it could possibly be claimed that a nation is treating its domestic currency more favorably. An investor may attempt to claim that a measure of this kind is in violation of fair and equitable treatment for reasons discussed above.

One window that would appear to be available to nations is the ability to tax capital inflows and outflows. Brazil taxed inflows of capital in late 2009, Malaysia taxed outflows in 1999. All US treaties have a chapter or series of paragraphs discussing taxation, saying that "nothing in Section A shall impose obligations with respect to taxation measures." Yet it distinguishes between traditional taxation and taxation that may be expropriating. Thus the evidence is not clear cut. In one of the numerous cases against Argentina in the aftermath of its crisis, an ICSID tribunal ruled that a tax on outflows was tantamount to an expropriation (Salacuse 2010).

It may be possible that a nation can claim that actions taken during a financial crisis are measures needed to protect the essential security of the nation. Language like Article 18 of the US Model BIT is found in most treaties:

> To preclude a Party from applying measures that it considers necessary for the fulfillment of its obligations with respect to the maintenance or restoration of international peace or security, or the protection of its own essential security interests. (United States of America 2004)

The article does not mention economic crises per se, but "all tribunals that have considered the matter thus far have interpreted the rules broadly enough to include such crises" (Salacuse 2010, 345). However, tribunals differ greatly over how grave the difficulties may be. In Argentina again, only one of three tribunals ruled that Argentina could not be held liable for actions it took to halt its crisis (Salacuse 2010). A key matter is whether or not a measure by a nation to stem a crisis can be seen as "self-judging." In other words, can the nation deploying the control be the judge of whether or not the measure taken was necessary to protect its security. The language quoted above in the 2004 Model BIT, which says "that *it* considers" is now seen as to mean that a measure is self-judging (because of the "*it*"), but Argentina's BITs with the US and others did not include as precise language at the time.

Finally, Article 20.1 of the 2004 Model BIT includes a provision on prudential measures that has almost the exact language found in the GATS under domestic regulations. It reads:

> Notwithstanding any other provision of this Treaty, a Party shall not be prevented from adopting or maintaining measures relating to financial services for prudential reasons, including for the protection of investors, depositors, policy holders, or persons to whom a fiduciary duty is owed by a financial services supplier, or to ensure the integrity and stability of the financial system. Where such measures do not conform with the provisions of this Treaty, they shall not be used as a means of avoiding the Party's commitments or obligations under this Treaty. (United States of America 2004)

This language is only to be found in the US–Rwanda BIT that is yet to be ratified, and not found in US FTAs. Regarding capital controls, the US government has stated that it is not its intention that controls be covered under this provision (United States Department of State (USDOS) Advisory Committee on International Economic Policy 2009). As discussed earlier, some have expressed concern that the last sentence of this paragraph may be self-canceling, others see it as quite flexible (Key 2003; Raghavan 2009; Stumberg 2009; Tucker and Wallach 2009; Van Aaken and Kurtz 2009).

US Investment Provisions versus Others by Major Capital Exporters

The investment provisions in US FTAs and of US BITs stand in stark contrast to the treaties of other major capital exporting nations. This section of the chapter reviews the measures in the OECD codes of liberalization, and some specific treaties by the EU, Canada, Japan and China.

OECD Codes

In many respects the OECD has the most expansive investment rules, as they cover all types of capital flows whether they are from the current or capital account. However, the OECD also has the broadest level of temporary derogations. Similar scope and derogation can be found in the OECD-sponsored Multilateral Agreement on Investment (MAI), which was never agreed upon. In terms of policy space for capital controls under the OECD Codes and the MAI:

- Members (OECD members) are expected to liberalize both the current and capital account.
- Members have a broad but temporary derogation where capital controls on both inflows and outflows are permitted.
- The OECD's draft MAI included a broad derogation analogous to that of the codes.

Incorporated in the early 1960s, two legally binding "codes" govern capital flows in OECD countries, the Code of Liberalization of Capital Movements and the Code of Liberalization of Current Invisible Operations – usually referred to as the Capital Movements Code and the Current Invisible Code. These codes cover all types of investments – inflows and outflows from the current and capital account – and require their liberalization.

Initially, speculative capital was excluded from the codes on grounds that short-term capital would disrupt the balance-of-payments position of OECD members and make it difficult for nations to pursue independent monetary and exchange rate policies. This was changed in 1989, when a group of nations led by the UK and Germany argued that all OECD nations by then had sophisticated enough money markets that they could withstand liberalization of short-term flows. All nations that acceded to the OECD since 1989, regardless of their level of development, also liberalized their capital accounts fully to include short- and long-term maturities. South Korea in its accession, however, argued that it should have a grace period to gradually open their capital account as they developed. The OECD denied this request, conditioning membership on an open capital account. In the end, South Korea conceded (Abdelal 2007).

Alongside the broad mandates for OECD countries there are also broad exceptions. Article 7 (in each set of codes) holds the "clauses of derogation," that govern the temporary suspension of commitments. Under these safeguards a nation may suspend liberalization. Article 7b allows a member to put in place temporary capital controls to stem what may "result in serious economic disturbance in the member state concerned, that member may withdraw those measures." Article 7c is the balance-of-payments exception: "If the overall balance of payments of a member develops adversely at a rate and in circumstances, including the state of its monetary reserves, which it considers serious that member may temporarily suspend the application of measures of liberalisation taken" (OECD 2009). Greece, Iceland, Portugal, Spain and Turkey have all used the derogation. The OECD permitted them to do so because these nations were seen to be at a lower stage of development relative to the other members of the OECD (Abdelal 2007).

The OECD-sponsored Multilateral Agreement on Investment was launched in 1995 as an attempt at a global treaty that would have similar provisions to the codes – for OECD and non-OECD (developing) countries alike. The draft text of that treaty included a broad safeguard for capital controls and other measures for balance-of-payments problem. In the end the MAI was abandoned in 1998 (OECD 1998).

BITs and FTAs for other major capital exporters

The EU, Japan, Canada and increasingly China are major capital exporters. Each of these capital exporters has numerous BITs and FTAs with nations across the world. And loosely, the BITs of these nations have the same general characteristics found in US BITs. However, in the case of the use of capital controls to prevent and mitigate financial crises, the BITs and investment provisions of all BITs and FTAs by these exporters either contain a broad "balance of payments" temporary safeguard exception or a "controlled entry" exception that allows a nation to deploy its domestic laws pertaining to capital controls.

Examples of the balance-of-payments approach can be found in the EU–South Africa and EU–Mexico FTAs (remember Mexico negotiated such a provision in NAFTA), the Japan–South Korea BIT, and the ASEAN agreements. The Korea–Japan BIT has language that clearly allows for restrictions on both inflows and outflows, presumably inspired by the 1997 crisis. The BIT states that nations may violate transfers provisions:

a. In the event of serious balance-of-payments and external financial difficulties or threat thereof; or
b. In cases where, in exceptional circumstances, movements of capital cause or threaten to cause serious difficulties for macroeconomic management, in particular, monetary or exchange rate policies. (Quoted from Salacuse 2010, 268)

Another way capital controls are treated by capital exporters in FTAs and BITs is referred to as "controlled entry" whereby a nation's domestic laws regarding capital controls are deferred to. Canada's and the EU's FTAs with Chile and Colombia each have a balance-of-payments safeguard *and* a controlled entry deferment (Canada Foreign Affairs and International Trade 2009). As an example of controlled entry, the investment chapter of the FTA between Canada and Colombia has an annex which states, "Colombia reserves the right to maintain or adopt measures to maintain or preserve the stability of its currency, in accordance with Colombian domestic legislation."

Controlled entry provisions are to be found in BITs as well. The EU does not sign many BITs as a union, but individual countries do. The China–Germany BIT states that transfers must comply with China's laws on exchange controls (Anderson 2009). In the case of China, that nation has to approve all foreign inflows and outflows of short-term capital (IMF 2009a).

Interestingly, EU member BITs vary a great deal. Some, like the China–Germany BIT and the UK–Bangladesh BIT allow for a nation to defer to its own laws governing capital controls. On the other hand, Sweden and Austria had US-style BITs with no exceptions whatsoever. However, the European Court of Justice ruled in 2009 that Sweden and Austria's BITs with several developing countries were in violation to their obligations under the EU treaty. While the EU treaty requires EU members to allow for free transfers, it also allows members to have exceptions. The court found that Sweden and Austria's treaties were incompatible with the EU treaty and that such treaties would need to be renegotiated to include exceptions to the transfer provisions (Salacuse 2010).

Echoing concerns expressed by the IMF earlier in the paper, host countries facing a diversity of commitments through different treaties can cause jurisdictional issues and cause economic distortions. The pending US–South Korea FTA is illustrative of the jurisdictional issue. If South Korea decided it needed to deploy controls on inflows as a prudential measure to prevent a crisis, they may have all the leeway to do so under the exceptions to the OECD codes, but not under the FTA with the United States. A conflict over which regime should prevail could arise. This could be further accentuated if the IMF was asked to conduct a country program for South Korea and advised the nation to deploy capital controls.

The US FTAs with Chile and Colombia just discussed are examples of potential discrimination problems. If Chile or Colombia wished to deploy a nondiscriminatory URR to all short-term capital inflows, the countries' treaty commitments would not permit the measures to be truly nondiscriminatory. Chile or Colombia would only be able to apply the measure to the EU or to Canadian firms and capital, not to capital flowing from the United States, thereby distorting capital markets and defeating the purpose of the nondiscriminatory prudential measure.

Returning to some of the key questions outlined above, the following can be said about the BITs and FTAs in relation to capital controls. The US holds 58 signed or pending BITs and FTAs with other countries. Almost all capital controls are actionable under these treaties. Recourse can be in the form of a one-time compensatory payoff.

Summary and Recommendations for Policy

This chapter has shown that that US trade and investment agreements, and to some extent the WTO, leave little room for deploying capital controls to prevent and mitigate a financial crisis. This is the case despite the increasing economic evidence showing that certain capital controls can be useful in preventing or mitigating financial crises. It also stands in contrast with investment rules under the treaties of most capital exporting nations.

That being said, there is room for developing countries to deploy capital controls to prevent and mitigate financial crises under the following circumstances:

- The controls are on capital transactions, not current transactions unless sanctioned by the IMF;
- The nation has not committed financial services under the GATS at the WTO;
- The nation does not have a BIT or FTA with the United States.

In terms of the WTO, close to one hundred nations have not made financial services commitments under the GATS and are therefore free to deploy whichever type of capital control on capital account transactions they see necessary. However, the 37 economies listed in Table 2.4 have made significant commitments on either Modes 1 or 3 for financial services and could be significantly vulnerable to actions against the use of capital controls.

Those nations that still retain the policy space to deploy capital controls and have not reached the threshold (identified by Kose et al. (2009), discussed earlier) necessary to withstand capital account liberalization should pursue Mode 1 (cross-border trade in financial services) commitments with caution in the Doha Round. As this chapter has shown, such commitments implicitly require an opening of the capital account. Moreover, those nations should exercise even more caution in terms of Mode 3 (FDI in financial services) commitments. The IMF study discussed in this chapter shows that those developing countries that liberalized FDI in financial services fared worse during the current crisis (IMF 2010). Regarding those nations that have already made commitments with respect to financial services under the GATS (the nations in Table 2.4), their only recourse will be the untested exceptions for prudential regulation and balance-of-payments exceptions.

Many nations fall under this category of course, including China, Brazil, India and others that frequently deploy capital controls either on a permanent or temporary basis to ensure macroeconomic stability. A more plausible option is reforming current and future agreements. Especially in the wake of the global financial crisis, nations should coordinate their policies so as to avoid discrimination and jurisdictional inconsistency. Based on the analyses in this chapter, there are five nonexclusive examples that the US could consider that would give nations the proper policy space for capital controls:

- Remove short-term debt obligations and portfolio investments from the list of investments covered in treaties. This has been raised as a possibility by actors ranging from the IMF to civil society (Hagan 2000; International Institute for Sustainable Development (IISD) 2005).
- Create "controlled entry" annexes in BITs and FTAs analogous to the Canada–Chile, Canada–Colombia, Chinese and EU agreements with those nations. Controlled entry grants a nation the full ability to use capital controls on capital account transactions as they see fit.
- Design a balance-of-payments exception that covers both inflows and outflows such as the provisions found in the Japan–South Korea BIT.
- Clarify that the essential security exceptions cover financial crises, and that measures taken by host nations are self-judging.
- Resort to a state-to-state dispute resolution process for claims related to financial crises, analogous to the WTO and the other chapters in most FTAs.

The last recommendation is an important one. Scholars argue that under a state-to-state dispute resolution system the state can take a much broader view regarding financial stability than an individual firm can. Whereas individual speculative firms may stand to lose from a capital control in the short term (unless their clients default of course), the net welfare benefits of a measure may be positive. The state is seen as being in a better position to "screen" for such benefits and also to weigh a dispute case against a variety of other geopolitical and economic concerns it may have with a host nation. Given that BITs and FTAs currently lack state-to-state dispute systems with appropriate screening mechanisms, some scholars predict that these will be used most by the private sector to file claims in response to measures taken to mitigate the global financial crisis (Van Aaken and Kurtz 2009).

Leading political scientists have been puzzled as to why the US continues its policy of capital account liberalization given the economic evidence, the treaties of its peers and given that it has been shown in the political economy literature that governments should favor capital controls (Alfaro 2004). Cohen (2007) attributes the US stance as a combination of ideology and domestic politics. Regardless of the party in power in the US, treasury officials and presidential advisors have largely held neoliberal training and beliefs. Perhaps more importantly, Cohen illustrates that while the costs of capital controls are directly felt by a handful of politically organized US constituents – Wall Street – the beneficiaries are diffuse and don't feel the direct effects. Thus a collective action problem persists where Wall Street organizes around capital account liberalization.

The arguments posed by the community lobbying against flexibilities for capital controls in the US are threefold. First, it is argued that capital controls simply don't work and that US treaties help nations get rid of suboptimal policy. Second, that such controls hurt US investors by restricting their ability to mobilize funds. Third, that changing our treaties would send a signal that earlier treaties are problematic and jeopardize commitments previously taken.

The evidence and politics may be changing. As discussed earlier in the chapter the evidence in favor of many capital controls is positive. Secondly, the current crisis has made it clear that while it is recognized that some individuals in the short term may incur damage, those damages may be minimal relative to what they could be under a crisis. Stability among our investment partners helps US investors and exporters have more certainty for markets. Crises could lead to defaults and large losses to US assets and export markets. And, crises can cause contagion that spreads to other US investment and export destinations. Third, the US may now be more sensitive given that it has taken numerous prudential measures in the wake of the current crisis – measures that may not survive the scrutiny of various trade and investment treaties with capital exporters who have investments in the US (Van Aaken and Kurtz 2009).

Chapter 3

THE NEW VULTURE CULTURE: SOVEREIGN DEBT RESTRUCTURING AND INTERNATIONAL INVESTMENT RULES

The global community still lacks a regime for sovereign debt restructuring, something that could have come in handy with the eurozone crisis. There is increasing concern that international investment agreements may become a "court" for sovereign workouts. Indeed, investment treaties between Argentina and European nations were used by European investors in an attempt to serve as a forum for settling debt disputes. Are international investment agreements the appropriate place for the global community to resolve sovereign debt restructuring in the event of a financial crisis? It has been often overlooked that the definition of a covered investment within international trade and investment agreements often includes sovereign debt. In lieu of this, this chapter analyzes the extent to which investment provisions in various treaties may hinder the ability of nations and private creditors to comprehensively negotiate sovereign debt restructurings when a debtor nation has defaulted or is close to default on its government debt. It is found that the treatment of sovereign debt varies considerably in terms of strength and applicability across the spectrum of now thousands of trade and investment treaties in the world economy. It is also found that most treaties may restrict the ability to restructure debt in the wake of a financial crisis. These findings could undermine the ability of nations to recover from financial crises and could thus broaden the impact of such crises.

Should Investment Treaties Govern Sovereign Debt Restructuring?

Government borrowing has been a feature of the world economy since the founding of nation-states, and a cornerstone of the growth and development process as well. Inevitably, however, with each financial crisis one or more nations find themselves restructuring or defaulting on their sovereign debt commitments.

Debt crises can be a function of government profligacy, unpredictable swings in global markets, or both. Although sovereign debt restructuring and default have been a constant feature of the global economy for centuries, the fact that there is not a comprehensive and uniform regime governing debt workouts has been seen as one of the most glaring gaps in the international financial architecture. The lack of a clear regime for restructuring has accentuated financial crises.

Does the incorporation of sovereign debt as a covered investment in some international investment agreements (IIAs)[1] hinder the ability of debtor nations and their creditors to work out their debt obligations in an efficient manner that facilitates economic development? This question has received relatively little attention in both the economic policy community focusing on financial crises and by the IIA community. The memory of the numerous defaults and restructurings in the 1990s, Argentina's restructuring after its crisis in 2001 and the current European crises have triggered a new wave of thinking regarding the interactions between financial crises and IIAs.

The central findings of this research are the following:

- Sovereign debt is often a covered investment under IIAs, thus
- Sovereign debt restructuring is seen as grounds for private bondholders to file arbitral claims under IIAs,
- If claims against sovereign debt restructuring become more widespread they could threaten the regime for financial crisis recovery that is already very fragile.

After exhibiting these findings, this chapter offers concrete measures to reform IIAs so their mission does not creep into financial crisis mitigation.

Debt, Development and Financial Crises

This section of the chapter provides a very brief overview of developing country debt problems and the current financial crisis and provides a critical review of the problems with the current regime for sovereign debt restructuring.

If managed appropriately, government borrowing can be an essential ingredient for economic development, and has been for centuries. Many developing countries have a savings gap – they lack the savings to finance planned investment, and thus seek to fill such a gap with domestic and foreign resources. If the gap is not reversed over time, however – if the ratio of exports to imports does not increase, if the rate of the return on development projects fails to exceed the interest rate on the debt, or if the nation's general stage of development does not equip it with the absorptive capacity to turn loans into successful income – then nations begin to see problems in servicing their debts.

Even when nations manage to circumvent such pitfalls, a nation could still spiral into a debt crisis – simply defined as when a nation that cannot (or is no longer willing to) service its debt. Contagion from other crises or herd-like bouts expressing a lack of investor confidence could prevent creditors from rolling over or increasing loans. Developing country debt is most often denominated in a foreign currency, so when interest rates rise or the value of a nation's currency falls, the cost of debt service can skyrocket (Eichengreen et al. 2005). When left unchecked, debt markets are too often procyclical – there is a lot of liquidity during boom times and thus nations tend to borrow, but liquidity dries up during recessions and can make it difficult for nations to rollover or increase debt (Minsky 1986). Even nations with low budget deficits can quickly be affected as governments borrow to stimulate an economy during a recession but then experience slow growth and low tax revenue thereafter. These tensions are exacerbated with developing nations that are overly exposed to international financial markets. Any number of the factors discussed above could cause massive inflows of debt and large swings in outflows that can cause financial instability (Herman et al. 2010).

The IMF found that 28 of the poorest nations have a high risk of debt crises in the wake of the financial crisis (IMF 2009b). Of course, the eurozone is already there. Many countries then, if not this time then the next, will need to reschedule, restructure or even default on their debt. At present there exists no adequate forum for nations to work out their debt problems.

From bailouts

Coordinated global bailouts have been part of the traditional response to prevent and mitigate debt crises, but receive a great deal of criticism because of their costliness and lack of effectiveness. In an attempt to prevent default, or to manage a recovery after such an event, nations are often granted "bailouts" in the form of new loans and grants from international financial institutions. Chief among those institutions is the IMF, but national governments and other institutions (such as the Paris Club) often contribute as well.

Increasingly however, bailouts are seen as unfair, providing the wrong incentives and lacking in effectiveness. The largest bailout until recently was the $50 billion rescue package for Mexico's crisis in 1994. Once seen as an unthinkable bailout, it has become eclipsed by the staggering $1 trillion for Europe's current crisis. These bailouts are often quickly re-sent out of the country to pay creditors and seldom help the nation regain its economic footing. Moreover, there is a question of fairness given that global taxpayers (through contributions to the IMF or their governments) are the ones footing the bill to foreign creditors. Critics also refer to the "moral hazard" problem that can come with international bailouts. If global investors (and debtors) know that they will be bailed out they will have the incentive to make evermore risky loans. Finally, the record on the effectiveness of bailouts is limited at best, with many nations taking years to recover, if at all (Eichengreen 2003).

To bail-ins?

Sovereign debt restructuring (SDR) is increasingly seen as an alternative to bailouts. However, the international community views the SDR regime to be greatly lacking. Many go so far as to argue that the lack of such an adequate regime to restructure sovereign debt in a comprehensive, fair and rapid manner is among most glaring gaps in the international financial architecture (Krueger 2002; Herman et al. 2010).

When a sovereign government is no longer willing or able to pay its debts, sovereign restructurings occur during what amounts to a formal change to debt contracts that is negotiated between creditors and debtors. SDRs (or "workouts") often take the form of reducing the face value of the debt, "swaps" where new bonds with lower interest rates and longer maturities are exchanged for the defaulted bonds, and so forth. Such workouts are usually highly discounted and result in a loss for bondholders. Losses or discounts are commonly referred to as "haircuts" (Sturzenegger and Zettelmeyer 2006). The process is often referred to as a "bail-in" because the participants are not outside of the investment itself as the IMF, governments and taxpayers are during a bailout. Table 3.1 lists some of the major SDRs over the last twelve years according to the duration of the SDR negotiations, the total face value of the bonds under restructuring, the "haircut" and participation rate.

It is held that a restructuring is deemed successful when 90 percent or more of bondholders participate in an offering that is no less than 50 percent on the net present value of the debt (Hornbeck 2010). There are always some "holdouts" during a restructuring, disgruntled investors that refuse to negotiate and demand the full value of their investment. These holdouts often file suits under the municipal laws that govern bond contracts in New York, London and beyond. There are also "vulture funds" that purchase debt when it is of a very low value before or after a restructuring then file suits to increase the value of their investment (Thompson and Runciman 2006). In a new development, and the subject of this chapter, holdout investors have filed claims under BITs and could potentially do so under numerous FTAs.

Despite some significant improvements, collective action problems and the lack of a uniform system continue to plague the SDR regime. SDRs are seen as

Table 3.1. Sovereign debt restructurings, 1998 to 2010

	Duration (m)	Value (USb)	Haircut (%)	Participation (%)
Russia (1998–2000)	20	31.8	37.5	98
Ukraine (1998–2000)	3	3.3	0	95
Pakistan (1999)	10	0.6	0	95
Ecuador (2000)	12	6.8	40	97
Uruguay (2004)	1	5.4	0	93
Argentina				
2005	40	81.8	67	76
2010	60	18	75	66
Argentina total	*100*	*99.8*		*93*

Sources: Porzecanski (2005), Dhillon et al. (2006), Hornbeck (2010).

strong alternatives to bailouts, at least in theory. Indeed, among the key rationales for efficient SDRs are the avoided costs of taxpayer funded bailouts and of the moral hazard associated with bailouts. Yet, the nature of private debt has evolved over time. For most of the twentieth century private debt was issued by large commercial banks. In a restructuring it was relatively easy for governments and international institutions to put pressure on a small number of such banks in order to facilitate a restructuring. However at the end of the century private debt became dominated by bonds which can be held by numerous holders. These holders can be dispersed across the globe and are hard to track down, thus making the restructuring process more complex (Eichengreen 2003).

Perhaps the most significant concerns relate to collective action problems that arise during a negotiation. Although a swift and efficient settlement could make creditors, debtors and international institutions better off, there are complex incentives that make negotiations drag on for long durations and can favor one party over another. Table 3.2 shows that even the shortest recent SDR took one month. And of course Argentina's debt wasn't restructured until 2010 – nine years of restructuring that still may not be over.

Eichengreen and Mody (2003) summarize the ramifications of a long and cumbersome restructuring process:

> Governments that default on their debts must embark on lengthy and difficult negotiations. Lenders and borrowers, uncertain of one another's willingness to compromise, may engage in costly wars of attrition, delaying agreement on restructuring terms. Even if disagreements about

the debtor's willingness and ability to pay are put to rest, dissenting creditors may continue to block agreement until they are bought out on favorable terms.

In the interim, the creditors receive no interest, and the borrowing country loses access to international capital markets. The exchange rate may collapse, and banks with foreign-currency-denominated liabilities may suffer runs. To avert or delay this costly and disruptive crisis, the International Monetary Fund will come under intense pressure to intervene, provoking all the controversy that IMF intervention typically entails. Officials of the borrowing country, for their part, will go to great lengths to avoid seeing the country placed in this difficult situation. They may raise interest rates, run down their reserves, and put their economy through a deflationary wringer, all at considerable cost to society. (80)

In addition to these problems, long workouts can accentuate debt overhang whereby a nation spends so much time and effort servicing its debt that a country cannot grow to its full potential (Rogoff and Zettelmeyer 2002).

These costs could be significantly reduced with a swift and orderly SDR process. A swift negotiation with standstills on payments and other measures to buffer a "rush to exit" in related assets would make all parties better off. Ironically, collective action problems get in the way.

It is in the interest of private creditors to support a regime that would prevent all creditors from rushing to exit (given that such a run would jeopardize the collective value of the asset) and keep a debtor solvent enough to pay debts. However, individual creditors have an incentive to quickly exit before other creditors do and still other investors may also hold out from negotiating until they are sure that the behavior of free riders that rush to exit is under control (Hagan 2005; Helleiner 2008). Of course it is in the debtors' interest to restructure debt in a manner that allows the nation to service its debt burden and begin to recover. Yet debtors have been reluctant to support a regime because they fear that the nation might be seen as more willing to default, resulting in a lack of general investor confidence in the country and a subsequent drain of investment (Helleiner 2009).

The rash of recent SDRs led to a near consensus that the SDR regime was in need of repair. By the turn of the century the international community was both fed up with IMF bailouts and frustrated with the SDR process. In 2001, Anne Krueger, a well-known US economist who had just taken the helm as the deputy managing director of the IMF, proposed a "Sovereign Debt Restructuring Mechanism" (SDRM). The SDRM was to be a new global mechanism analogous to bankruptcy courts for private creditors (known as Chapter 11 in the US). The argument for the SDRM was that it would minimize the need for major taxpayer and IMF bailouts to private creditors and reduce the moral hazard problem. The main features of the SDRM (outlined in Table 3.2) were:

- A payments standstill on bonds, and capital controls, all to be monitored by the IMF;
- A stay on litigation altogether or at least the requirement of a supermajority (75 percent) approval of stays on litigation;
- A process would also enable the process to prioritize some loans over others and for new loans to be made by the IMF and others; and
- A supermajority of among all bondholders regardless of a particular bond issue, would be all that was needed to accept the terms of the restructuring (Hagan 2005).

Table 3.2. Varieties of debt workouts

	Runs	Holdouts	Prioritizing loans	Supervision
Chapter 11	Standstills	Supermajority voting Litigation stay	Preferred status for new money	Court supervision
SDRM	Standstills Capital controls	Supermajority voting Litigation stay	Preferred status for new money	Neutral agency plus IMF program
CACs		Supermajority voting		Representation clauses
Result	Unilateral standstills Capital controls	CAC (supermajority voting) ICSID	Unilateral	Bond swaps/ exchanges

Source: Author's adaption from Miller (2002) and Herman et al. (2010).

The SDRM was vehemently opposed by private creditors, the US government and even some creditor nations. As Helleiner (2009) and Setser (2010) explain, the US government did not want to grant the IMF so much power and did not want to engage in dollar diplomacy across the world. Private creditors argued that the status quo was not a bad one. Although there was a theoretical discussion of the collective action problem just described, creditors noted that no restructuring had been held up due to litigation. Some debtors were concerned that they would not receive any more IMF support, and were concerned that they would be scorned by private investors in the marketplace.

US deputy treasury secretary John Taylor proposed an alternative that has ended up becoming fairly widespread. Taylor proposed a more market-based "contractual" approach whereby bonds themselves would have collective action clauses within their contracts. Most bonds issued from London at the time included such clauses, but most US bonds did not. The key features of collective action clauses (CACs) are that they:

- Have a *collective representation* component where a bondholders meeting can take place where creditors exchange views and discuss the default/restructuring;
- *Minumum enforcement* component whereby 25 percent of the bondholders must agree that litigation can be taken;
- *Majority restructuring* components that enable a 75 percent supermajority of bondholders to bind all holders within the same bond issue to the terms of restructuring;

This idea has really taken off and at this point CACs are found in more than 90 percent of newly issued bonds in the United States (Helleiner 2009).

Although CACs are a significant improvement, they are still seen as lacking by many observers. First, bondholders can be globally dispersed, as opposed to the day when a handful of major banks could be rounded up. Many bonds are also sold on secondary markets, making it even more difficult to "call a vote." Second, for some bond issues it may be easy for holdouts to purchase a 75 percent majority for a vote and neutralize the collective action component of the issue. In other words, it may not be very difficult to prevent 75 percent of the bondholders from accepting a restructuring, and/or to prevent just 25 percent of bondholders from voting to move to litigation. Third, and even more concerning, is what is called the "aggregation problem." CACs only cover individual bond issues but have no effect on the holders of other issues. Restructurings increasingly involve multiple bond issuances and CAC provisions do not hold for collective action across multiple issuances (the SDRM would have allowed for such a mechanism) (Hagan 2005). To be clear, CACs cover a single bond issuance. Say, for example a 10 month bond issued by country X in 2008. Country X may issue a 15-year bond in 2009, with a CAC as well. Often however, when a nation restructures they restructure multiple bond issuances. While CACs work within a particular bond issue, they do not cover multiple bonds. If bondholders of some issues refuse a government's offer, they may have to be paid in full. Moreover, a debtor may have fewer resources to share with other issue holders, who may then reject its restructuring offer (Eichengreen and Mody 2003, 80).

The most recent restructurings have occurred in Argentina, culminating in 2010. A short synopsis of the Argentina case is featured in Box 3.1. There have been holdouts in Argentina's restructurings, some of whom have gone to ICSID under a BIT.

Box 3.1. Argentina: Crisis, default, restructuring and ICSID

In June of 2010, Argentina may have completed the most controversial sovereign default in history. Argentina restructured $100 billion of debt three times between 2001 and 2010.

During the 1990s Argentina was seen as the poster child of the Washington Consensus. In addition to major privatizations, trade and investment liberalization, and a general reduction of the state in economic affairs, Argentina enacted a "convertibility plan" that laid the foundation for the crisis to come. In a nutshell the convertibility plan guaranteed a one-to-one convertibility of the peso to the US dollar and capped the ability of the nation to print domestic currency at the amount of US dollars held in reserve (Blustein 2005). To carry out the plan fiscal and monetary policy had to be tight because the government could not expand the money supply to fill budget gaps – thus leaving austerity or borrowing as the only options for preserving the system.

The plan got off to a positive start but convertibility and an open capital account left the nation open to external shocks. When the crises of the late 1990s in Asia and Russia spread to Brazil and led to a depreciation of the Brazilian real, Argentina was faced with competitors with weaker currencies – in an environment of a rising dollar, of falling commodity prices, and a retreat from emerging market investment. Rather than warning Argentina of its eroding position, the IMF continued to support Argentina's policies (Damill et al. 2010). A debate rages regarding the relative importance of each of these factors, but it is clear that by 2001 the Argentine economy ran out of steam and the country defaulted in January of 2002. GDP fell by 10 percent that year and poverty doubled.

For years new policymakers in Argentina attempted to negotiate a restructuring under the supervision of the IMF. By 2004 Argentina had decided to take a different route. Argentina announced that it would open a one-time bond exchange and passed domestic legislation that it would never hold a future swap with a better offer. In January of 2005 the country opened an exchange on over $100 billion in principal and interest on a diverse number of bond issuances whereby the bondholders were to receive a 67 percent haircut. In the end it restructured just over $62 billion with a 76 percent participation rate (24 percent holdouts).

Holdouts and some observers of the restructuring were furious, going so far to call Argentina a "rogue creditor" (Porzecanski 2005). Some holdouts, among them numerous vulture funds, took the litigation route in the United States, where 158 suits have been filed (Hornbeck 2010).

For the first time ever, a number of those holdouts filed claims under IIAs to the International Centre for the Settlement of Investment Disputes (ICSID). In September 2006, approximately 180,000 Argentine bondholders filed a claim under the Italy–Argentina BIT for approximately $4.3 billion. The creditors claim that the Argentine restructuring was tantamount to expropriation and violated fair and equitable treatment standards under the treaty (Waibel 2007).

Argentina was still left with a significant debt load and was shy of the 90 percent threshold for the restructuring to be seen as successful such that the rest of the holdouts could essentially be ignored. Argentina launched another take-it-or-leave-it exchange from May to June of 2010 for $18 billion of its debt – offering a staggering 75 percent haircut under the same rationale as in 2005, despite experiencing a recent boom (Porzecanski 2010). As was the case with the 2005 swap, the bonds were exchanged for bonds with CACs and that are linked to GDP – the bonds pay out more when the economy is growing fast, and less during slower times. Sixty-six percent of the bondholders ($12.1 billion) tendered. $6.2 billion worth of bondholders will continue to litigate either through domestic courts or through ICSID. It does appear, however, that some of the Italian bondholders who have filed an ICSID claim did indeed tender, though $1.2 billion or more remain with their ICSID claim (IMF 2010; Hornbeck 2010). Nevertheless, the two swaps together now amount to 92 percent of bondholders tendering, what is normally seen as successful enough for Argentina to move on. Do the ICSID cases change this? In August 2011, ICSID ruled that ICSID had jursdiction over the Argentina case. This decision greatly facilitates lawsuits under IIAs to frustrate sovereign restructuring by states (ICSID 2011).

The recent case with Argentina reveals that the regime for SDR remains far from adequate. Argentina has been shunned by international capital markets for almost nine years during the process, and creditors took heavy haircuts. Costly to all involved, except for perhaps the patient bondholders who have turned to ICSID. To this issue we now turn.

Sovereign Debt Restructuring and International Investment Agreements

This section of the chapter examines the extent to which various trade and investment agreements grant developing nations the policy space to restructure sovereign debt in a comprehensive, just and efficient manner. Significant inconsistency is found regarding the coverage of sovereign debt in various trade and investment regimes. When sovereign debt is covered in a treaty, however, a number of concerning questions arise.

The scope, coverage and jurisdiction of IIAs vary widely (Salacuse 2010). To what extent is sovereign debt covered and when covered under what provisions might an investor have grounds to file a claim because of restructuring? The following areas are discussed in this section: jurisdiction, umbrella clauses, national treatment, fair and equitable treatment, expropriation, transfers, and safeguards. Each of these areas will be briefly discussed in turn.

Jurisdiction

Many IIAs treat "any kind of asset" as a covered investment and therefore include sovereign bonds. More recent treaties explicitly list bonds as covered by the treaty. That said, there are numerous treaties that do not include sovereign debt as well.[2] Other treaties do not include portfolio investment at all.[3] Increasingly, however, sovereign bonds are included in IIAs. This leads to two concerns that are addressed in this subsection: the increasing coverage of sovereign debt in IIAs and the extent to which CACs provide protection under IIAs.

In terms of general jurisdiction and coverage, an arbitration claim against sovereign debt restructuring depends on several issues: whether the tribunal finds that it has jurisdiction, which requires there to have been an *investment*; and *consent* by the sovereign party or a claim based on the investment agreement itself. In terms of jurisdiction, the consent of the sovereign party is governed by the investment agreement. This is where the "definitions" provisions of IIAs come in. If an agreement clearly includes bonds and other debt instruments as covered investments, then the country has consented to jurisdiction for those claims. By extension, then, any limitation within the BIT (such as the safeguarding annexes and the general exclusion in NAFTA of sovereign debt claims discussed later) to those claims is a limitation on consent (Cross 2006). Indeed, an August 2011 ICSID case ruled that an IIA had jurisdiction over sovereign restructuring in the case of Argentina (ICSID 2011). Analysis of BITs and FTAs for this chapter reveals that almost all of the agreements by major capital exporters (OECD nation's treaties) include "any kind of asset" as covered investments and thus likely cover sovereign bonds. Some treaties, such as NAFTA, the majority of Peru's IIAs and in some others (such as the Australia–Chile FTA) exclude or safeguard sovereign debt.

It appears that CACs do not provide adequate protection for sovereign debtors in terms of IIAs. On the surface, CACs would appear to prevent holdouts of sovereign bonds and vulture funds from filing claims under IIAs. Yet even if the bondholders of a particular issuance voted against litigation through a minority clause or agreed to the terms of a restructuring under a majority clause, such actions under a CAC would *not* prevent an investor from filing an arbitral claim. According to Waibel (2007), CACs cover contractual rights of enforcement under municipal laws and are not designed to deal with treaty claims. Thus even if a CAC was deployed, holdout bondholders could file a treaty claim arguing that the terms of a treaty have been violated. This leads Waibel to say that "ICSID arbitration could blow a hole in the international community's collective action policy" (Waibel 2007, 715). Waibel expands:

> The prima facie limited coverage of CACS – their failure to include arbitration – opens up a new window of opportunity for holdout litigation. The importance of this potential loophole for sovereign debt markets cannot be overemphasized. Consider the following scenario.
>
> ICSID tribunals could conceivably hear treaty claims concerning sovereign bonds despite the legitimate exercise of CACS, which would become ineffective in binding nonparticipating creditors. If CACs were to leave treaty claims untouched, then they would bar only contractual causes of action originating in the bond contract. Bondholders might be able to obtain compensation even through the contractually prescribed majority of bondholders accepted the sovereign debt restructuring. Recourse to ICSID arbitration could thus create a legal gap in the international community's collective action policy. (Waibel 2007, 736)

Furthermore, bondholders could "treaty shop" and file claims under treaties where it may be more certain that a bondholder will win jurisdiction (Wells 2010). Waibel (2011) has pointed out that a great deal of sovereign bonds are traded on secondary markets and nationality can literally change in a matter of minutes, accentuating the ability of a nation to "shop" for favorable treaties.

Umbrella clauses

Umbrella clauses, when they appear in IIAs, are intended to "impose an international treaty obligation to host countries that requires them to respect obligations they have entered into with respect to investments protected by the treaty. This places such obligations under the "umbrella" of international law, not just the domestic law that would otherwise apply exclusively." (Salacuse 2010, 275). Thus, a host state has the responsibility to respect both its treaty obligations in addition to, or even despite the fact, that the same obligations may also be governed by domestic laws and contracts. This makes the host state subject to the jurisdiction of investor-state arbitration. Therefore, contractual approaches to SDR such as CACs could be interpreted as being within the scope of an IIA, via an umbrella clause. Even if a bond issuance with a CAC has had a bondholders meeting whereby a supermajority has agreed to accept the restructuring and if there was not a minimum enforcement vote of 25 percent of bondholders to litigate, under an umbrella clause holdouts may still be able to resort to investor-state arbitration.

National treatment

National treatment implies that foreign investors are treated no less favorable than their domestic counterparts. Domestic investors have been treated differently under some restructurings, with considerable economic justification, and could thus trigger claims under IIAs. Put simply, a national treatment claim could occur when a foreign bondholder receives different terms during a restructuring than do domestic holders.

Economists who specialize in mitigating financial crises agree that there are numerous circumstances when domestic investors should be given a priority over foreign creditors. As countries liberalize their capital accounts the line between external and domestic debt becomes blurred. In years past it was relatively easy to delineate between external and domestic debt. In a nutshell, external debt was issued in foreign currency and was held by foreigners and domestic debt was denominated in local currency and held by residents. Under a liberalized capital account foreign investors may invest in domestic debt and domestic residents may purchase foreign debt. Indeed, domestic financial institutions and residents held close to half of Argentina's debt that was restructured between 2001 and 2010. Economists and prominent legal scholars alike conclude that "the ability to treat domestic and foreign creditors differently is a necessary policy option for governments in a financial crisis," (Gelpern and Setser 2004, 796).

The economic (and political) rationale for treating domestic and foreign investors differently during a debt crisis is multipronged. First, it is recognized that domestic investors are often hit by a "double adjustment" during a crisis and restructuring. Domestic investors not only suffer the reduction in the value of their bonds through the restructuring, but they are also affected by the impact of post-crisis ramifications that could include slow growth, high unemployment, high interest rates and devaluation. On the other hand, foreign investors' commitments will be in their own currency and these investors will not be affected by the domestic effects because they are outside the country in question and are very unlikely to make continued investments in the host economy in the short term (Caliari 2009).

On a related note, prioritizing domestic debt may be in order so as to revive a domestic financial system, provide liquidity and manage risk during a recovery. Without such measures a banking crisis can ensue where massive outflows of foreign exchange and/or bank runs can occur. In both the Russian and Argentinean cases domestic investors received more favorable treatment with this in mind (Panizza 2010; Gorbunov 2010; Gelpern and Setser 2004; Blustein 2005; IMF 2002).

Politics also plays a key role. The support of important constituents and political groups is often essential for a recovery and reform effort to be successful. There is also a clear rationale to prioritize the citizenry through maintaining the ability of economic actors to pay wages, salaries and pensions in order to maintain livelihoods, enable domestic demand and avoid mass protest (Gelpern and Setser 2004; IMF 2002).

Expropriation

Sovereign debt restructuring or default could be interpreted as constituting a direct or indirect expropriation. It is held that among the claims levied by Italian bondholders under the Italy–Argentina BIT is the alleged expropriation of their investments through restructuring. Expropriation is commonly defined and seen in IIAs as "wealth deprivation" where "substantial deprivation" occurs that could be *direct* where an investment is "taken" in the form of a title or physical seizure, or indirect whereby the title or physical nature of the investment is not changed, but its value may be diminished (OECD 2004). Both defaults and restructuring obviously diminish the value of an asset, and under a "take-it-or-leave-it" swap arrangement a bondholder has the choice to either lose a bond altogether or to accept a new bond with a haircut. Tribunals often perform a "substantial deprivation" test to examine the level of diminished value in a restructuring, and would thus in this case be examining the size of the haircut in a bond exchange (Newcomb and Paradell 2004).

Fair and equitable treatment

Most newer IIAs include a "fair and equitable treatment" (FET) clause that usually grants investors the rights to transparency, protection of investors' reasonable expectations, freedom from harassment and coercion, due process and good faith (Waibel 2007). Legal scholars have expressed concern that restructuring in general and bond exchanges in particular can be seen as violations of FET.

Concern has been expressed that bond exchanges may violate FET in and of themselves, despite the fact that exchanges have become standard practice for restructurings. Waibel (2007) outlines a number of justifications for claiming that bond exchanges violate FET under IIAs. Waibel sees it as possible that exchanges could trigger allegations that the process lacks transparency and is coercive. In addition, the "take-it-or-leave-it" nature of exchanges could be seen as violating due process and not seen as being in good faith given that the government does not take part in serious restructuring negotiations. Finally, Waibel also sees restructuring as possibly seen as actionable because a restructuring may be seen as transforming the business environment or undermining the legal framework of the bonds themselves.

Transfers

The transfers clauses in IIAs increasingly require that all covered investments of participating parties be transferred "freely and without delay." Restructuring could potentially clash with transfers provisions on three levels. First, an outright default ceases the transfer of the bond in question and thus could be seen as a clear violation. Second, during the restructuring negotiations presumably little transferring related to the bonds in question is occurring and could possibly be grounds for disgruntled investors to file (or threaten to file to speed negotiation) a claim. Third, under some of the proposals for the SDRM, the IMF or another body would hold a "standstill" during the negotiations whereby the nation deploys temporary capital or currency controls during the negotiations. In one of the numerous cases against Argentina in the aftermath of its 2000–2001 crisis, an ICSID tribunal ruled that a tax on outflows (a common form of capital control used during crisis by Malaysia as well) was a violation of the transfers and expropriation clauses (Salacuse 2010).[4]

Safeguards

To what extent might defaults and restructuring be protected under the various forms of safeguard clauses that can be found in many IIAs? Key safeguards that may provide cover are "essential security" provisions as well as special annexes in a handful of US IIAs.

It may be possible that a nation can claim that actions taken during a financial crisis are measures needed to protect the "essential security" of the nation. Language like Article 18 of the United States Model BIT is found in many treaties:

> [...] to preclude a Party from applying measures that *it considers* necessary for the fulfilment of its obligations with respect to the maintenance or restoration of international peace or security, or the protection of its own essential security interests. (USTR 2004)

The article does not mention economic crises per se, but "all tribunals that have considered the matter thus far have interpreted the rules broadly enough to include such crises" (Salacuse 2010, 345). However, tribunals differ greatly over how grave the difficulties must be. In Argentina again, only one of three tribunals ruled that Argentina could not be held liable for actions it took to halt its crisis. A key matter is whether or not a measure by a nation to stem a crisis can be seen as "self-judging." In other words, can the host nation using the control be the judge of whether or not the measure taken was necessary to protect its security. The language quoted above in the 2004 Model BIT, which says "that *it* considers" is now seen as to mean that a measure is self-judging (because of the "*it*"), but Argentina's BITs with the United States and others did not include as precise language at the time (Salacuse 2010).[5]

In addition to self-judging, states often have to show there is a "necessity defense" in order to invoke essential security exception – a defense that is strictly delimited in customary international law. The word "necessary" was also used in the BIT clause. As such Argentina and other nations facing crises will have to demonstrate that its measures were "necessary" to address a threat to its essential security. Tribunals have to decide how much suffering and destitution a state is expected to tolerate in the welfare of its population and condition of its economy before one is prepared to conclude that it is necessary to intervene in spite of the state's obligations to foreign creditors, investors and so forth.

Annexes on sovereign debt restructuring in US IIAs

Some of the recent IIAs negotiated by the United States clearly define sovereign bonds as covered investments and provide explicit guidelines for the interaction between SDR and certain IIAs. What is found in the US–Uruguay BIT and in FTAs with Central America, Chile, Peru and Colombia is a special annex on sovereign debt restructuring. Though the specific text varies across the treaties with such an annex, such provisions usually prohibit claims against "negotiated debt restructuring," unless an investor holds that a restructuring violates national treatment (NT) or most favoured nation (MFN) status. Such treaties usually define "negotiated restructuring," as a restructuring where 75 percent

Table 3.3. Sovereign debt restructuring annexes in recent US IIAs

	US–Chile FTA 2003	US–Uruguay BIT 2006	DR–CAFTA 2005	US–Peru 2007	US–Colombia Pending
Definition of "investment"	Includes loans, bonds	Includes loans, bonds	Includes loans, bonds	Includes loans, bonds	Includes loans, bonds
Safeguard for restructuring	Yes	Yes	Yes	Yes	Yes
NT and MFN exception to safeguard	Yes	Yes	Yes	Yes	Yes
"Negotiated" restructuring requirement	No	Yes	No	Yes	Yes
"Cooling off" period	No	For *non-*negotiated restructuring, except for violations of NT and MFN, 270 days	No	For *non-*negotiated restructuring, except for violations of NT and MFN, 270 days	For *non-*negotiated restructuring, except for violations of NT and MFN, 270 days

of the bondholders have consented to a change in payment terms. If an investor does file a claim in the event of a restructuring that is not a "negotiated" one, s/he must honor a "cooling off" period usually lasting 270 days before a claim may be filed. There is no cooling off period for a non-negotiated or negotiated restructuring that violates NT or MFN. The agreements with such provisions are contrasted in Table 3.3.

It should be noted that such annexes are not standard in US treaties after NAFTA (NAFTA excludes sovereign debt from the definition of investment altogether). Indeed, the US–Australia, US–South Korea, US–Morocco, US–Oman, US–Panama and US–Singapore agreements included bonds and debt as covered investments but do not include annexes for sovereign debt restructuring. The absence of such a safeguard in the US–South Korea agreement is striking given the memory of that nation's historic crisis in the 1990s (Blustein 2001).

The US was initially very reluctant to include such annexes in its agreements. According to interviews with US negotiators for this report the US does not initiate discussions regarding sovereign debt, but only responds to them when raised by negotiating partners. The US, however, sees SDR as not being much of a problem with IIAs at this point because of the emergence of CACs. The annexes on SDR are regarded by the US as being designed to raise the comfort level of trading partners concerns.

The first nation to express concern over IIAs and SDRs was Chile, during the US–Chile FTA negotiations. The text for the resulting annex can be found in Box 3.2. The second was the US–Uruguay BIT; according to Uruguay's chief negotiator who was interviewed for this chapter, Uruguay was unaware of Chile's measures. The Uruguay BIT is the first to introduce the "negotiated restructuring" requirement and the "cooling off" period. US–Chile (and later US–DR–CAFTA) ban claims during a restructuring regardless of the type of restructuring except when a restructuring violates NT or MFN clauses but do not refer to a "negotiated restructuring."

The negotiations with Uruguay took place in 2004, just months after Uruguay restructured its debt. Uruguayan negotiators wanted to make sure that the BIT recognized as lawful what Uruguay had just done and that, more importantly, it allowed for that kind of flexibility in the future should a similar circumstance arise. According to interviews with negotiators, the US at the beginning was strongly opposed to the idea. This was a deal breaker for Uruguay. After a year of back and forth the US finally came around. Uruguayan negotiators report that this was the toughest issue and the last one to be resolved.

To summarize then, under the Uruguay/Peru/Colombia agreements, any country can engage in a "negotiated restructuring" without being liable to losses of foreign investors. Under these same agreements, however, non-negotiated restructuring is subject to claims as long as the investor waits 270 days (the same in each agreement) from the event before filing the claim.

Implicitly in the Uruguay BIT and more explicitly in the Peru and Colombia agreements, NT and MFN claims may be brought regardless of whether the restructuring is negotiated and regardless of the cooling off period. In all these cases, the annex excludes Articles 3 and 4 (NT and MFN) from its safeguard umbrella.

The Dominican Republic–Central America FTA resembles the Chile FTA much more closely. Like the above agreements, bonds and other debt instruments are considered covered investments under the agreement. Annex 10-A, then specifies very clearly that sovereign debt restructuring is subject *only* to Articles 10.3 (National Treatment) and 10.4 (MFN). The additional cooling off period does not seem to apply and there is no mention of "negotiated restructuring" as a prerequisite.

Box 3.2. US–Chile FTA and DR–CAFTA

Annex 10-B
Public Debt

The rescheduling of the debts of Chile, or of its appropriate institutions owned or controlled through ownership interests by Chile, owed to the United States and the rescheduling of its debts owed to creditors in general are not subject to any provision of Section A other than Articles 10.2 and 10.3.

US–Peru and US–Colombia Free Trade Agreements

Annex 10-F
Public Debt

1. The Parties recognize that the purchase of debt issued by a Party entails commercial risk. For greater certainty, no award may be made in favor of a claimant for a claim under Article 10.16.1(a)(i)(A) or Article 10.16.1(b)(i)(A) with respect to default or non-payment of debt issued by a Party unless the claimant meets its burden of proving that such default or non-payment constitutes an uncompensated expropriation for purposes of Article 10.7.1 or a breach of any other obligation under Section A.
2. No claim that a restructuring of debt issued by a Party other than the United States breaches an obligation under Section A may be submitted to, or if already submitted continue in, arbitration under Section B if the restructuring is a negotiated restructuring at the time of submission, or becomes a negotiated restructuring after such submission, except for a claim that the restructuring violates Article 10.3 or 10.4.
3. Notwithstanding Article 10.16.3, and subject to paragraph 2 of this Annex, an investor of another Party may not submit a claim under Section B that a restructuring of debt issued by a Party other than the United States breaches an obligation under Section A (other than Article 10.3 or 10.4) unless 270 days have elapsed from the date of the events giving rise to the claim.

Limits of the US approach

These annexes can be seen as a step in the right direction given that parties to the agreement recognize that restructuring is a special case, yet they remain far from adequate for at least four reasons. First, as summarized in Box 3.3, CACs will not alleviate the possibility that nations will seek claims for restructuring. As indicated earlier, vulture funds and other holdouts can acquire a supermajority within a bond issuance and neutralize the bond issue and a 25 percent minority can still agree to litigate and arbitrate. Second, the definition of investment and umbrella clauses allow for investor-state arbitration over treaty obligations regardless if such obligations are also covered by local law. Third, most restructurings are multi-issue restructurings and suffer from the aggregation problem described above. Again, collective action clauses only apply within a bond issue, not across multiple issues that are often bundled together in a restructuring.

Box 3.3. Collective action clauses and IIAs: Three problems

---

1. Holdouts can acquire a supermajority within a bond issuance and neutralize the bond issue and a 25 percent minority can still agree to litigate and arbitrate.
2. "Definitions" of investment and umbrella clauses allow for investor-state arbitration over treaty obligations regardless if such obligations are also covered by local law.
3. Many sovereign debt restructurings involve numerous bond issues and suffer from the agglomeration problem – collective action clauses do not apply across bond issuances, only within single bond issuances.

Fourth, economists and international financial institutions have repeatedly held that there are numerous circumstances when national treatment should be violated. Economic policymakers will often treat domestic bondholders and financial institutions differently during a crisis. Prioritizing domestic debt may be in order so as to revive a domestic financial system, provide liquidity and manage risk during a recovery (Gelpern and Setser 2004, 796). Third, take-it-or-leave-it bond exchanges such as those that have occurred in Argentina would satisfy the 75 percent rule, but it is not clear that such swaps could justly be deemed as "negotiated."

Summary and Conclusion

This chapter has shown that the regime for effective sovereign debt restructuring is very fragile and the ability of holdout bondholders to use IIAs to reclaim the full value of their bonds could further undermine the development of an effective regime for sovereign debt restructuring.

Sovereign debt restructuring by definition changes the investment environment, reduces the value of an investment, allows a host government to "take" back some of a loan and often results in bonds held by domestic financial institutions and citizens being restructured differently than those of foreign bondholders. When sovereign debt is defined and "covered" by an IIA then, numerous conflicts could arise between SDR and IIAs.

Argentina is thus far the only nation to be subject to IIA claims related to the nation's default and subsequent restructuring. Creative holdouts have sought ICSID claims because of that restructuring and ICSID has just ruled that it has jurisdiction over restructuring.

It thus appears that investor-state claims through IIAs are now an avenue for holdout bondholders to attempt to claim the full value of their original investments. Such action could accentuate collective action problems because private creditors may have a disincentive to vote to accept a restructuring because those holders going to ICSID have rushed to do so.

The United States is the only nation that includes explicit provisions regarding SDR in a small handful of its IIAs. While a step in the right direction, such provisions may prove to be inadequate in the event of an SDR. The annexes for SDR in US IIAs do not permit SDR that violates national treatment, among other measures. It has long been held in the crisis management community that domestic interests need to be treated differently than foreign interests in response to a crisis, including in a restructuring. Such a spirit is clearly violated when US investors can resort to national treatment to file claims during a restructuring. Given that the United States is now the largest debtor nation and the value of that debt could drastically be affected in the event of a default or a stiff rise in interest rates, the US may be at a point when it too should reconsider how deep the coverage of sovereign debt in its IIAs should be.

The following are a handful of nonexclusive policy remedies that would enable IIAs to grant nations the policy space to conduct effective SDRs in the future:

- **Exclude sovereign debt from IIAs**. The exclusion of sovereign debt from "covered" investments under future treaties would relegate sovereign debt arbitration to national courts and to international financial bodies. Many IIAs already exclude sovereign debt, such as NAFTA and others. Argentina's new model BIT is reported to be moving in this direction as well.
- **Clarify that mitigating crises is "essential security."** Clarify that the essential security exceptions cover financial crises and that sovereign debt restructuring taken by host nations is "self-judging" and of "necessity."

- **Create safeguards for SDR**. A handful of recent IIAs have included explicit provisions regarding SDR. While this is a positive development, for reasons discussed in this chapter such provisions may not prove to be fully adequate.
- **State-to-state dispute resolution for SDR and crisis** related instances may be more prudent given that governments need to weigh a host of issues in such circumstances. States attempt to examine the economy-wide or public welfare effects of crises whereas individual firms rationally look out for their own bottom line. Investor-state tips the cost-benefit upside down, giving power to the "losers" even when the gains to the winners of an orderly restructuring may far outweigh the costs to the losers.

This list of reforms is by no means a final one, nor is this chapter the end of discussion on this subject. The global financial crisis that began in 2008 has triggered a discussion on the proper forums for preventing and mitigating financial crises. It is hoped that this chapter contributes to that discussion.

Notes

1 "IIA" in this chapter refers to any agreement with international investment provisions, therefore including both bilateral investment treaties (BITs) and free trade agreements (FTAs).
2 Canada–Colombia FTA (2008), Article 838, footnote 11; Australia–Chile FTA (2008), Article 10.1(j)(iii); Azerbaijan–Croatia BIT (2007); Chile–Japan FTA (2007), Article 105. Recently revised model BITs of Colombia (2008) and Ghana (2009) exclude sovereign debt.
3 Turkey Model BIT (2009), Article 1(1).
4 *El Paso Energy Internacional Company vs. Argentina* (ICSID Case No. ARB/03/15), Decision on Jurisdiction (27 April 2006).
5 *Continental Casualty vs. Argentina* dismissed most, but not all, of the claimant's claims on the basis of the essential security exception. The Sempra Energy International vs. the Argentine Republic annulment panel annulled the Sempra award on the basis that it demonstrated a manifest excess of powers because, although it dealt with the issue of whether Argentina could justify its measures under customary international law it did not address whether the measures could be justified under the BIT security exception. The CMS vs. Argentina annulment panel found a similar failing by the original tribunal to explain why it concluded that the essential security exception would not apply to the emergency measures in question, but declined to annul the award on the grounds that the failings did not rise to the level of a "manifest" excess of powers.

Chapter 4

WHITHER THE DEVELOPMENTAL STATE? INDUSTRIAL POLICY AND DEVELOPMENT SOVEREIGNTY

With Rachel Denae Thrasher

This chapter examines the extent to which the emerging world trading regime leaves nations the "policy space" to deploy effective policy for long-run diversification and development and the extent to which there is a convergence of such policy space under global and regional trade regimes. We examine the economic theory of trade and long-run growth and underscore the fact that traditional theories lose luster in the presence of the need for long-run dynamic comparative advantages and when market failures are rife. We then review a "toolbox" of policies that have been deployed by developed and developing countries past and present to kickstart diversity and development with the hope of achieving long-run growth. Next, we examine the extent to which rules under the World Trade Organization, trade agreements between the European Union and developing countries, trade agreements between the United States and developing countries, and those among developing countries (South–South, or S–S, agreements) allow for the use of such policies. We demonstrate that there is a great divergence among trade regimes over this question. While S–S agreements provide ample policy space for industrial development, the WTO and EU agreements largely represent the middle of the spectrum in terms of constraining policy space choices. On the far end, opposite S–S agreements, US agreements place considerably more constraints by binding parties both broadly and deeply in their trade commitments.

Introduction

Development is a long-run process of transforming an economy from concentrated assets based on primary products, to a diverse set of assets based on knowledge. This process involves investing in human, physical and natural capital in manufacturing and services and divesting in rent seeking, commerce and unsustainable agriculture (Amsden 2001). Imbs and Wacziarg (2003) have confirmed that nations that develop follow this trajectory. They find that as nations get richer, sectoral production and employment move from a relatively high concentration to diversity. They find such a process is a long one and that nations do not stabilize their diversity until they reach a mean income of over $15,000. For many years it has also been known that as countries diversify they also undergo a process of deepening whereby the endogenous productive capacities of domestic firms are enhanced through forward and backward linkages (Amsden 2001; Krugman 1995; Hirschman 1958).

This chapter examines the extent to which the emerging world trading regime leaves nations the "policy space" to deploy effective policy for long-run diversification and development, and the extent to which there is a convergence of such policy space under global and regional trade regimes. The first part of the chapter examines the economic theory of trade and long-run growth and underscores the fact that traditional theories lose luster in the presence of the need for long-run dynamic comparative advantages and when market failures are rife. We then exhibit a "toolbox" of policies that have been deployed by developed and developing countries past and present to kick start diversity and development with the hope of achieving long-run growth but also stress that tools alone are not the recipe for development, that "getting the political economy right" is also of vital importance. In the second part, we examine the extent to which rules under the WTO, trade agreements between the EU and developing countries, trade agreements between the US and developing countries, and developing country–developing country trade agreements (South–South) allow for the use of such policies. The final part of the chapter summarizes our findings and offers conclusions for policy and future research. This chapter is intended to assist policymakers as they choose trade partners that affect their ability to design long-run development strategies.

Trade theory and the long run

The traditional trade theory that provides the backdrop and justification for the majority of trade treaties is limited in terms of long-run growth for developing countries. Such theories assume a static approach to technological change and assume that there are no market failures among trading partners, two assumptions that do not hold in the developing country context (Caves et al. 2007). This section of the chapter provides an overview of trade theory and its limitations and shows how some countries have used various tools to correct for the theoretical limitations identified.

Neoclassical trade theory demonstrates that liberalizing trade can make all parties better off. The economist David Ricardo (1911) showed that because countries face different costs to produce the same product, if each country produces and then exports the goods for which it has comparatively lower costs, then all parties benefit. The effects of comparative advantage (as Ricardo's notion became called) on factors of production were developed in the "Heckscher–Ohlin" model (Ohlin 1967). This model assumes that in all countries there is perfect competition, technology is constant and readily available, there is the same mix of goods and services, factors of production (such as capital and labor) can freely move between industries, and there are no externalities. In other words, this model is "static" and not "dynamic" and there are no market failures.

Within this rubric, the Stolper–Samuelson theorem adds that international trade can fetch a higher price for the products (and hence lead to higher overall welfare) in which a country has a comparative advantage (Stolper and Samuelson 1941). In terms of FDI, multinational corporations moving to another country can contribute to development by increasing employment and by human capital and technological "spillovers" where foreign presence accelerates the introduction of new technology and investment (Jyaraman and Singh 2007). In theory, the gains from trade accruing to "winning" sectors freed to exploit their comparative advantages have the (Pareto) possibility to compensate the "losers" of trade liberalization. Moreover, if the net gains from trade are positive there are more funds available to stimulate growth and protect the environment. In a perfect world then, free trade and increasing exports could indeed be unequivocally beneficial to all parties.

To some, static comparative advantage poses problems for countries who want to sustain long-run growth. Some countries may only have a static comparative advantage in a single commodity where prices are very volatile and where longer-run prices are on the decline relative to industrial goods. What's more, small initial comparative static advantages among countries in the short run may expand into a growing technology gap between rich and poor nations in the longer run (Lucas 1988). If the developed world has a static comparative advantage in innovation, it can continually stay ahead by introducing new products, even if the developing world eventually catches up and gains a comparative advantage in low-cost production of each old product over time (Krugman 1979).

In the longer run then, what matters most is not static comparative advantage at any one moment in time, but the ongoing pattern of dynamic comparative advantage: the ability to follow one success with another, to build on one industry by launching another, again and again. Since the process of technology development is characterized by increasing returns, many models will have multiple equilibria. It is easy to specify a model in which the choice between multiple equilibria is not uniquely determined by history; rather, it becomes possible for public policy to determine which equilibrium will occur (Krugman 1991). If, in such a model, the multiple equilibria include high-tech, high-growth paths as well as traditional, low-growth futures, then public policy may make all the difference in development.

Neoclassical trade theory also assumes that there are no market failures among trading partners (Caves et al. 2007). However, four key market failures plague nations seeking to catch up to the developed world; coordination externalities, information externalities, dynamic technological change, and human capital formation (Kumar and Gallagher 2007). "Diversification by definition can mean the creation of whole new industries in an economy and sometimes may require linking new industry to necessary intermediate goods markets, labor markets, roads and ports, and final product markets. For fifty years economic theorists have demonstrated how markets fail at 'coordinating' these efforts. Coordination failures and the asymmetric distribution of world income has led economists to argue that the nation-state should provide 'big push' investments to build scale economies and enhance the complimentary demand and supply functions of various industries" over the long run (Kumar and Gallagher 2007, 7).

While historically such efforts took the form of large industrial planning efforts and infant industry protection, more recently industrial clustering has taken place where nations focus on the development of specific technologies or sectors in specific geographical regions – especially when facing scale economies. Clustering and export processing zones have been created to attract foreign firms, link them to domestic input providers and serve as exporting platforms. To support these efforts, nations (most successfully in Asia) provide tax breaks and drawbacks to foreign firms but require them to source from domestic firms and transfer technology (Amsden 2001). In tandem, the state provides an educated labor force, public research and development, tariff protection, subsidized credit to support the domestic firms and provided export subsidies to the domestic firms until they could produce products at the global technological frontier (Murphy et al. 1989; Weiss 2005).

Markets also fail at providing the socially optimal amount of "information" to producers and consumers as well – such phenomena are termed information externalities. Technological experimentation through research and development and the inquisitive process of entrepreneurship involve a process of "self-discovery" regarding which economic activities and product lines will be the most appropriate for a domestic economy (Rodrik 2007, 105). These experimenters who tinker with establishing or inventing new technologies to adapt to local conditions provide enormous social value to a national economy but solely bear the course of failure (and success). These entrepreneurs need to be compensated for their experimental nature through subsidization of exports and credit, temporary tariff protection, patent rewards and marketing support. Without such incentives, entrepreneurs will be more apt to invest in historically profitable industries in the primary product sectors (Krugman 1995; Hirschman 1958; Gerschenkron 1966).

As hinted earlier, related to coordination and information externalities is that trade liberalization and comparative advantage tends to produce static gains, but make dynamic gains through technological change more elusive. The static models of the gains from the trade suggest that a country such as Brazil should dismantle its industrial sector in favor of specializing in soy and meat production, and that India should de-emphasize services and heavy manufacturing in favor of textile and apparel specialization (Ackerman and Gallagher 2008; Anderson and Martin 2005). These models, if deployed 20 years ago, would have told South Korea and China to focus on rice production. However, following the lead of Japan, the United States and Europe before them, many nations in East Asia and Latin America fostered more diversified and higher value added sectors over time (Chang 2002; Okimoto 1989). Thirty-five years ago if South Korea and China had relied on comparative advantage we might not be driving Kias and Hyundais, using Haier appliances or typing on Lenovo laptops.

In enabling the technological capacity of new industries, markets do not give the correct investment signals when there are high and uncertain learning costs and high levels of pecuniary externalities.[1] In other words, technological dynamism that leads to diversification is not guaranteed by market reforms alone. For many of the reasons described earlier – weak capital markets, restrictive intellectual property laws, lack of information and poor coordination, imperfect competition and the need for scale economies – underinvestment in technologically dynamic sectors can occur (Lall 2005; Nelson and Winter 1982; Arrow 1962). Historically, to correct for these market failures nations have encouraged joint venturing through technological transfer agreements with foreign firms to learn technological capabilities. In addition they have invested heavily in higher education and publicly funded research and development (Amsden 2001). What is more, nations have selectively loosened intellectual property rules to allow for learning and supported innovative firms through government procurement, export subsidies, subsidized capital and tariff protection (Amsden 2001; Chang 2002).

Although mentioned in each of these previous examples, human capital formation is also essential for dynamic economic growth and diversification (Grossman and Helpman 1991). Once again, private markets fall short of supplying human capital at a socially optimal level. There are numerous arguments why markets undersupply education and that governments should intervene to increase the supply of educated workers. Basic literacy and education have positive externalities such as improved health and better participation in democratic processes – in other words the social rate of return on education is higher than personal investment (Friedman 1962). With respect to learning in private firms, firms may underinvest in the training of their workers because of fears of high labor turnover (Rodrik 1992). The Four Asian Tigers – like developed countries before them – spent a great deal of effort providing education and training to their people. This was done by spending a significant amount of funds on education (including providing scholarships to obtain PhDs in developed countries), clustering schools in export processing zones, requiring that foreign firms hire nationals and train them on the job and subsidizing training programs in domestic firms (Lall 2000). Table 4.1 exhibits an illustrative (but far from exhaustive) list of trade and industrial policies used by East Asian and other developing economies over a 40-year period and the market failures such policies address. It is this list of policies that will be expanded upon and analyzed in the following section.

Table 4.1. Tools for correcting market failures

Market failure	Policy instrument
Coordination failures	Tariff sequencing
	Tax drawbacks
	Infrastructure provision
Information externalities	Administrative guidance
	Subsidized credit/entrepreneurship
	Tariff sequencing
	Patent restrictions
Scale economies/technological dynamism	Tariff sequencing
	Technology transfer requirements
	Joint ventures
	Public research and development
	Compulsory licensing
	Patent restrictions
	Government procurement[2]
Human capital formation	Public education
	Local labor requirements
	Movement of people

Source: Kumar and Gallagher (2007).

Getting the political economy right

Some countries have been fairly successful at deploying policies to create dynamic comparative advantages and to correct for market failures. In the developing world, the recent standouts are Taiwan, South Korea and more recently China. Table 4.2 exhibits average annual growth rates in GDP per capita for selected regions of the world from 1960 to 2005.

Table 4.2. Growth in GDP per capita for selected regions, 1960 to 2005

	1960–1980	1980–2005	2000–2005
High income	5.7	2.1	2.8
East Asia and Pacific	3.5	6.6	7.2
China	3.4	8.6	8.6
Latin America and the Caribbean	2.9	0.5	1.4

Source: World Bank (2008).

Today's developing nations look to these success stories as possible models for twenty-first-century policy. East Asia experienced 3.5 percent annual per capita income growth from 1960 to the 1980 and 6.6 percent since 1980 – one of the most impressive growth trajectories on record. What is more, such growth has also corresponded with reduction in inequality and improvements in many other social indicators. It is beyond the scope of this chapter to explain in detail the literature on development in these nations, but experts attribute East Asian growth to four general categories of policies (World Bank 1993; Amsden 2001; Lall 2000):

- **Targeted industrial policy** with reciprocal control mechanisms where nations selectively secluded certain industries where they wanted to gain dynamic comparative advantages;
- **Loose intellectual property rules** where nations encouraged learning from foreign nations through government research and development efforts and at times reverse engineering goods from foreign counterparts;
- **The movement of people across borders** for higher education and temporary work. The best students were sent to the US and Europe to earn degrees in science, mathematics and technology then came home to work in targeted industries or government;
- **Investment in human capital and public infrastructure** where governments invested heavily in education and provided infrastructure such as roads, ports and so forth.

There is considerable debate regarding the extent to which these policies were the key drivers of growth in some countries. Nevertheless, at this point there is widespread agreement that these policies did have *some* positive effect on economic performance. The debate now centers on what level of effect that was (World Bank 1993). It is not the purpose of this chapter to enter that debate. Nor is it the purpose of this chapter to judge the value of those policies for development. Rather, based on the evidence that such policies have had some positive effect, this chapter examines whether developing countries are still given (or keeping) the choice to deploy them under existing and proposed trade rules.

Whereas the East Asian nations – such as South Korea and Taiwan – managed their integration into the world economy through gradual liberalization and some degree of government involvement, nations in Latin America and the Caribbean (LAC) rapidly liberalized their economies in a short period of time – along the lines currently being advocated in the Doha Round. As we see in Table 4.2 for LAC, income growth since liberalization began in the 1980s has been barely one percent annually.

Many economists have expressed caution over advising other developing countries to follow the same path as East Asia. First, governments can be pathetic in picking "winners" for industrial policy. Many governments have tried to adopt proactive policies and have failed miserably – in other words, meeting market failures with government action often leads to government failure (Noland and Pack 2003). Governments have been criticized for not being able to pick winning sectors to focus on. Indeed, there are many examples of governments picking "losers." South Korea and Taiwan are often cited as success stories but Indonesia, Nigeria and Brazil have had failures that have received less attention in scholarly circles (Evans 1995; Burton 1983). In addition, subsidization and government involvement has been shown to accentuate "rent-seeking" behavior that make it additionally difficult for developing country governments to let go of projects that aren't going well or that have already reached maturity (Krueger 1996).

Market failures are not always easy to identify and once they are identified it isn't just a matter of pulling out a policy toolbox, grabbing a tool from one of these lists and hammering away. Indeed, while there is a strong theoretical justification for proactive government policy, development success takes much more than the proper rationale and proper policies. Development success stories from the twentieth century all struck a unique blend between state and markets – they got the *political economy* of industrialization right.

These critiques are quite valid. Without the proper political economy conditions, government intervention can create more problems than they correct. However, the most successful cases in large part circumvented these problems because governments designed policies where state actors were "embedded" in the private sector and where the state enforced discipline on the private sector. We refer to these phenomena as "embedded diagnostics" and "reciprocal control mechanisms."

By definition, the presence of market failures demonstrates the inability of the private sector to interpret the signals and trends it faces in the economy. If firms right in the middle of the marketplace cannot always make the best decisions about products and processes, why should governments make better decisions (Burton 1983)?

To circumvent the "picking winners" problem, political economists have shown that successful industrializers have had states that were "embedded" in the private sector while maintaining "autonomy" from sectional elite interests seeking rents. State agencies that are charged with correcting market failures have to maintain constant communication and input with the private sector (Evans 1995). Such public–private partnerships help both sectors "discover" what the most pertinent market failures and other impediments to industrial development are in an economy, what assets there are in the economy that can be built upon, and to pick activities that will have the largest economy-wide effects (Rodrik 2008).

Having a good toolkit and embedded autonomy is still not enough. In fact, public–private partnerships could become marriages of corruption and rent-seeking. Successful industrial policy has also tamed the tendency of rent seeking. In order for this to work, industrial policy has to be coupled with a good deal of discipline and accountability for both private actors and the state. Alice Amsden (2001) has referred to the need for "reciprocal control mechanisms." A control mechanism is "a set of institutions that disciplines economic behavior based on a feedback of information that has been sensed and assessed" (Amsden 2005, 221–2). For the East Asian success stories, the key principle behind their use of control mechanisms was "reciprocity:"

Reciprocity disciplined subsidy recipients and thereby minimized government failures. Subsidies were allocated to make manufacturing profitable – to convert moneylenders into financiers and importers into industrialists – but did not become giveaways. Recipients of subsidies were subjected to monitorable performance standards that were redistributive in nature and result-oriented. The reciprocal control mechanism thus transformed the inefficiency and venality associated with government intervention into collective good. (Amsden 2005, 222)

In other words, firms have performance requirements that when they are not met lead to a termination of supporting benefits by the state. The most successful industrializers were able to abandon projects that were not performing whereas others where perpetuated because bureaucrats became hijacked by business interests who became dependent on the state. Since public policy may make a difference in development, and, in fact, has been used successfully by some developing nations to increase diversification and related growth, it is important to understand the extent to which such policy space exists today.

Testing for Policy Space in the WTO and Beyond

Of the historical tools for diversity and development, which ones remain available under the new global trading regime? Do bilateral and regional agreements further limit policy space for development? This chapter examines four trade-related areas (goods, services, investment and intellectual property) across three agreement models. By comparing US-style, EU-style and South–South agreements with the WTO trade disciplines we determine to what extent the various regimes constrain policy space for member nations. In so doing we draw important lessons from the different trade agreement models and evaluate which are best for the purposes of promoting sustainable development in the long run.[3]

Table 4.3. Illustrative toolbox flexibilities

Policy instrument	WTO and associated agreements[4]	US agreements	EU agreements	South–South agreements[5]
Tariff sequencing	√	X	X	√
Tax export incentives	√	X	√	√
"Non-tariff barriers" in services	X	X	X	√
Movement of natural persons	√	X	√	√
Public education	√	√	√	√
Local labor requirements	√	X	√	√
Technology transfer	√	X	√	√
Domestic content[6]	X	X	X	√
Infrastructure provision	√	√	√	√
Administrative guidance	√	√	√	√
Subsidized credit/ entrepreneurship	√	√	√	√
Patent restrictions by origin/industry/ duration	X	X	X	X
Compulsory licensing	√	√+	√	√

Table 4.3 expands the illustrative list of development policy tools in Table 4.1 in the first column and then indicates whether such policies are permitted under various trading arrangements. A "√" signifies that yes the measure is permitted; an "X" denotes that a measure is not permitted. We go into this table in greater detail below, but an initial examination reveals that some models provide considerably more policy space for member countries.

Policy space also varies across issue areas. In the following pages, we first discuss the role that bilateral and regional agreements play within the multilateral trading system. We then examine the policy space available in each of four issues: trade in goods, trade in services, investment protection and intellectual property. Although the agreement models are by no means homogenous, we hope to draw some general conclusions about which trade agreements best promote long-term development.

Bilateral agreements in the multilateral system

Since the signing of the General Agreement on Tariffs and Trade in 1947, member countries have attempted to establish a baseline of liberalization for global trade in goods. The creation of the World Trade Organization in 1994 expanded that vision to cover trade in services, intellectual property and a host of other sub-issues related to trade (WTO 2012b). Alongside of the multilateral trading system, countries have clamored to sign bilateral and regional accords, broadening and deepening their commitments to trade liberalization (Carpenter 2009). For that reason, most (though not all) FTAs and customs unions (CUs) exceed the disciplines of the WTO.

The most favored nation (MFN) clause, requiring that WTO members treat all other members as their most favored trade partner, would seem to make bilateral agreements moot (GATT 1947, Art. I). However, Article XXIV of the GATT, as well as Article V of the GATS make room for these agreements so long as they liberalize "substantially all" trade in goods and services. By fully liberalizing trade between partners, proponents of the multilateral trading system hope that the agreements will act as building blocks toward multilateral free trade.

WTO oversight has met with very limited success, however. Of the hundreds of agreements notified, only one has ever been deemed to meet the terms of Articles XXIV and V (Fiorentino et al. 2009). Still, most agreements do exceed the WTO in both breadth and depth. US-style agreements, traditionally the most uniform and comprehensive model, govern everything from goods and services trade to investment protection, intellectual property and domestic regulation among others (for example, DR–CAFTA 2004; NAFTA 1993; US–Chile 2003; US–Singapore 2003). EU-style agreements tend to depend more on the trading partner. While EU–Chile (2002), EU–Mexico (2000,

2001) and the more recent EU–CARIFORUM (2008) agreements resemble the US model, EU–South Africa (1999) and EU–Tunisia (1998) cover less ground, omitting such issues as financial services, electronic commerce, and labor and the environment.

The 1979 GATT decision on "differential and more favorable treatment" (the "Enabling Clause") makes more room for lesser developed countries (LCDs) to sign bilateral accords without demanding reciprocity or liberalization of "substantially all" trade, as Article XXIV requires. Today, many developing countries enter into FTAs and CUs under the Enabling Clause in order to retain extra flexibility in complying with WTO standards. In part for that reason, many South–South agreements seem skeletal in comparison with the North–South models. The South Asian Free Trade Agreement (SAFTA), for example, effectively contains commitments only in the area of goods trade. On the other hand, the Southern Cone Common Market (MERCOSUR) and the Andean Community of Nations (CAN) cover as many issues as some EU agreements.[7] Still, broader issue coverage does not always signify deeper trade commitments. Likewise, depth of coverage within these agreements can act as much to protect developing economies from the outside as to liberalize within. In the following pages, we explore how differences in agreement breadth and depth affect the policy flexibility that countries enjoy within the global trading system.

Goods trade policies

Countries have employed many policies affecting trade in goods to promote growth and development. Here we explore the flexibilities still available to member countries under bilateral and multilateral trade arrangements, looking specifically at tariff barriers, non-tariff barriers, export incentives and safeguards. Table 4.4 provides a brief overview of the policy space available under the WTO and two North–South trade agreement models.

Table 4.4. Goods checklist

Policy instrument	WTO and associated agreements	US agreements	EU agreements
Tariffs	√	X	X
Quantitative restrictions/licensing	X	X	X
Tax drawbacks/deferrals and EPZs	√	X	√
Safeguards for injurious imports and balance of payments[8]	√	√	√
Safeguards for shortages[9]	√	X	√

Tariffs

Tariffs have long been the preferred trade barriers under the WTO and its predecessor and underlying agreement, the GATT, because they are easy to measure, transparent to apply and straightforward to liberalize progressively over time. Employed carefully, countries can raise and lower tariffs to protect nascent industries until they are ready to face global competition (Chang 2002). The WTO implicitly permits such measures, allowing countries to bind their tariff rates at or below the current applied rates – giving little or no room for adjustments upward.[10] Table 4.5 provides an example, comparing bound and applied rates for photographic paper in rolls wider than 610 mm.[11]

Table 4.5. Illustrative tariff comparison: Photographic paper, in rolls wider than 610 mm (%) (HS8 37031000 or equiv.)

Country/agreement	WTO binding	Bilateral agreement binding	MFN applied rate (avg.)
Chile: US and EU	25.0	6.0	6.0
Mexico: US and EU	35.0	0.0[12]	11.5
Costa Rica: DR–CAFTA	45.0	10.0	9.0
Nicaragua: DR–CAFTA	40.0	5.0	10.0
Honduras: DR–CAFTA	35.0	10.0	10.0
Guatemala: DR–CAFTA	45.0	10.0	10.0
Dominican Republic: DR–CAFTA	35.0	8.0	8.0
US–Singapore	6.5	0.0	0.0
EU–Tunisia	38.0	0.0	15.0
EU–South Africa	15.0	0.0	5.0

Sources: WTO 2009; EU–Chile 2002; US–Chile 2003; EU–Mexico 2000; NAFTA 1993; DR–CAFTA 2004 (individual tariff schedules); US–Singapore 2003; EU–Tunisia 1998; EU–South Africa 1999.

Non-tariff barriers

In addition to tariffs, countries have employed other trade restrictions (non-tariff barriers or NTBs) to protect domestic industry and promote development. Unlike tariffs, however, all modern trading regimes strongly disapprove of NTBs, generally prohibiting quantitative restrictions (quotas), import licensing, and import and export price requirements (Bhala 2003). Under the WTO, however, countries may introduce NTBs to address food shortages and balance-of-payments difficulties, or to enforce certain local standards and regulations (GATT 1947, Art. XII).[13]

EU-style agreements generally mimic WTO standards and incorporate both the balance-of-payments and shortages exceptions for imposing NTBs. Still, EU treaty language tends to vary with the treaty partner. EU–CARIFORUM (Art. 240), for example, contains an exception for balance-of-payments difficulties, but none for shortages. Meanwhile, EU–Tunisia (Art. 19) and EU–South Africa (Art. 19) expressly prohibit only quotas. US-style agreements likewise mirror the WTO standard for NTBs. Few US-style FTAs, however, make the same room for exceptional circumstances. Only one of six treaty partners under DR–CAFTA retained a shortages exception, and most recent agreements have eliminated the exception for balance of payments (Art. 3.8(2)).[14]

Incentives for export

Another way countries have encouraged development is through export incentive programs to reward companies, industries and even regions for export performance (Balassa 1978).[15] Taking the form of duty drawbacks, tax deferrals and export processing zones (EPZs), these measures can promote a healthy trade balance and enable local industry to compete globally (Rhee 1985). The WTO places no restraints on export incentive policies and seems to prefer them to more direct subsidy programs (SCM 1994).[16] Likewise, EU agreements incorporate the WTO standard here, omitting explicit discipline on the subject.[17]

The US model, on the other hand, almost universally prohibits such incentives.[18] Under NAFTA, member states may not provide drawbacks or tax deferrals on condition that goods are exported or used as material for another exported good (Art. 303). US–Chile and DR–CAFTA, also prohibit new or continuing duties waivers based on certain "performance requirements," which include export level or percentage requirements as well as other production performance measures (US–Chile 2003, Art. 3.8; DR–CAFTA 2004, Art. 3.4).[19]

Safeguards

Despite the controversy surrounding the Special Safeguard Mechanism for agriculture at Doha, the WTO actually retains a fair amount of safeguard flexibility for countries facing sudden injurious levels of imports, balance-of-payments difficulties and critical food shortages. Under the WTO, countries may address these problems temporarily by imposing NTBs, suspending tariff concessions or raising tariff rates (GATT 1947, Arts XII:1; XIX:1(a)).

Based largely on the WTO model, EU agreements provide the same flexibilities for countries addressing harmful levels of imports, balance-of-payments difficulties and, in some cases, shortages (EU–Chile 2002, Arts 92, 93, 195; EU–Mexico 2000, Arts 15, 16, 21).[20] Taking it a step further to promote development, some EU treaties also permit transitional safeguards, which may be imposed solely to protect infant industry (EU–Tunisia 1998, Art. 14; EU–South Africa 1999, Art. 25).

Once more, US agreements close in on the policy space otherwise available, not allowing safeguard measures in the case of shortages.[21] The agreements also do not allow countries to introduce new NTBs as safeguard measures and they require that, in the case of injury by imports, the imports not only *cause serious injury or threat thereof* (GATT language), but that they be the *substantial* cause of that injury – a higher legal standard (US–Singapore 2003, Art. 7.1; US–Chile 2003, Art. 8.1; DR–CAFTA 2004, Art. 8.1; NAFTA 1993, Art. 801).[22]

North–South models and South–South responses

North–South trade agreements generally constrain policy space more tightly than the WTO and its associated agreements. However, some developing countries have begun to make their own room for public policy by joining together to form South–South trading blocs that leave open even more policy options for diversification and development. Some South–South agreements, for example, allow member countries wholesale exceptions to the general liberalization program. These "sensitive lists" are often safe from both tariff concessions and the elimination of NTBs.[23] Furthermore, by excluding certain issues, such as taxes, from the agreement terms, South–South arrangements make room for members to provide export and other incentives.[24]

Notably, these agreements disfavor safeguards except in "exceptional cases" and limit their use to situations with injurious levels of imports. Lesser-developed countries seem to worry that industrialized trade partners would use safeguards against them, injuring their exports. SAFTA hints at this concern by making a special consideration for lesser-developed members, limiting safeguards against them (Art. 16.8).

Since 1994, global trade disciplines have increased in scope to cover services trade regulation, treatment of foreign investment and intellectual property protection, among others. The following sections explore these trade-related policy areas and the extent to which trade agreements impact policymakers' decisions today.

Trade in services

Since the Uruguay Round, global trade in services has increased drastically. Some of the fastest growing sectors such as computer-related services, legal services and advertising and technical service jobs grew between 70 and 250 percent from 1994 to 2004. Of 54 bilateral and regional agreements with services trade provisions, only five predate the Uruguay Round. Prior to the formation of the WTO, countries retained substantial freedom in regulating services trade so long as the measures didn't interfere with goods trade as well. Today, however, the new multilateral trading system and bilateral agreements circumscribe their efforts to varying degrees. Table 4.6 compares the policy space available for certain measures affecting services trade. In the following discussion, we detail the practical constraints that today's trade agreements place on member country governments.

Table 4.6. Services checklist

Policy instrument	WTO and associated agreements	US agreements	EU agreements
Control over sensitive sectors[25]	√	√	√
Non-tariff barriers in services	X	X	X
Duty of establishment	√	X	√
Withholding right of establishment	√	X	X[26]
Domestic regulation[27]	√	√	√
Movement of natural persons	√	X	√
Investments in public education	√	√	√

Sensitive sectors

Many countries have retained control over sensitive sectors such as "essential services, network infrastructure services and financial services" within their economy in order to promote economic stability (ActionAid et al. 2008). Theoretically, countries may continue to protect these sectors under any FTA through the negotiation process. However, the process differs significantly depending on the trade agreement model. The WTO adopts what has been called a "positive-list approach," meaning that protection is the rule rather than the exception (Marconini 2006). Thus, unless the country specifically commits a sector, it remains unbound. The WTO's General Agreement on Trade in Services also permits LDCs to liberalize later and carve out public services from coverage so that they are not bound by the rules of the agreement (Arts IV, XIX).[28]

Like the GATS, EU agreements have adopted a positive-list approach (EU–Mexico 2001, Art. 7; EU–Chile 2002, Art. 99; EU–Tunisia 1998, Art. 32.1 EU–South Africa 1999, Art. 29.1).[29] Some EU agreements pronounce a general standstill on future measures inconsistent with liberalization, indirectly binding even unbound sectors. However, recent agreements such as EU–CARIFORUM do not contain such a clause, indicating that standstill provisions may not become a permanent trend in EU–style treaties (ActionAid et al. 2008). The pivotal difference between the US model and GATS-based models is found in the negative list approach to liberalization – making protection the exception rather than the rule (Marconini 2006). Practically speaking, this means that countries must negotiate for every sector they want to protect – a highly negotiation intensive process.

In theory, US agreements permit countries to make reservations to the MFN principle, to reserve room for future measures that are inconsistent with liberalization and to protect whole sectors from the agreement. These options seem unavailable under an EU or WTO framework (NAFTA 1993, Art. 1206; DR–CAFTA 2004, Art. 11.6; US–Chile 2003, Art. 11.6; US–Singapore 2003, Art. 8.7). Both EU-style agreements and the GATS expect eventual full liberalization across sectors (GATS 1994). If such comprehensive liberalization results, developing countries that seek multilateral or EU-style trade preferences for the policy flexibility they provide may end up with more restraints than they bargained for, 20 or 30 years down the road.

"Non-tariff barriers" in services: Quota equivalents for services trade

Just as in goods trade, countries have introduced quantitative and qualitative restrictions on trade in services to promote domestic industry and control the behavior of service suppliers. For the most part, these measures are no longer permitted under any international trading regime. GATS provides a template for such restrictions, prohibiting service supplier quotas, transaction or asset restrictions, output quotas, employment limitations, organization-type requirements (such as joint ventures) and limitations on foreign capital participation by any means (GATS 1994, Art. XVI). Only in sectors where countries did not make market access commitments do they have policy flexibility. The same applies to US and EU-style agreements. Some employ GATS-equivalent language (EU–Chile 2002; EU–Mexico 2001; EU–CARIFORUM 2008; US agreements),[30] while others simply incorporate the terms of GATS by reference (EU–Tunisia 1998, EU–South Africa 1999).

Two differences stand out between the trade agreement models, however: the binding approach and the type of agreement coverage. As mentioned above, under the GATS and EU treaties, countries must specifically bind sectors to market access rules, while the US model binds all sectors except those expressly excluded. More importantly, the US model regulates foreign capital participation and joint ventures under the investment chapter rather than the services section of the agreement. Since the investment chapter is not sector-specific, it binds even more broadly than the US's negative list approach to service commitments.[31]

Duties and rights of establishment

Policymakers have also introduced policies influencing establishment rights to control the quantity and quality of service suppliers. A duty of establishment,[32] forces service suppliers to establish a local place of business or become a resident in order to provide their service (for example, NAFTA 1993, Art. 1205). By contrast, a "right of establishment" provides foreign services suppliers with a presumptive right to establish themselves in the partner countries.

The text of the GATS mentions neither a duty nor a right of establishment for foreigners. At the same time, specific commitments by some countries maintain a duty of establishment in certain sectors. In bound sectors, such measures would likely have to be set out in the schedule for continued liberalization (Marconini 2006). EU-style agreements look much like the GATS with regard to maintaining an establishment duty; however, they vary widely in their treatment of establishment *rights* (ActionAid et al. 2008). EU–Chile (Art. 132), for example, mandates national treatment with respect to establishment, for both legal and natural persons of agreement partners. The agreement with Mexico (2001, Art. 12) provides an express right of establishment for financial service suppliers only. Meanwhile, EU–CARIFORUM (Art. 109(5)) carves out a narrow right of establishment for maritime services.[33]

Unlike the GATS and EU agreement models, the establishment commitments in US agreements are neither sector- nor partner-specific. Countries that partner with the US may not impose any duties on foreign services suppliers or investors to establish a local commercial presence (NAFTA 1993, Art. 1205; DR–CAFTA 2004, Art. 11.5; US–Chile 2003, Art. 11.5; US–Singapore 2003, Art. 8.6).[34] Likewise, they must extend a universal right of establishment to all US legal entities who desire entry into their country (for example, DR–CAFTA 2004, Art. 10.3). The standardized US approach, therefore, allows little wiggle room for countries seeking policy options for development.

Domestic regulation

Possibly one of the most domestically invasive and yet universally accepted provisions in trade agreements addresses the issues of domestic regulation of service suppliers. As countries have expressed concern that their trading partners would use regulation as veiled discrimination, the GATS, followed by regional and bilateral agreements, imposes some limits on the use of domestic regulation.

The GATS spells out the universal standard for balancing legitimate regulation with trade liberalization: that general policy measures are administered reasonably, objectively and impartially, that the regulations are based on "objective and transparent criteria [...] not more burdensome than necessary [...] [and] not in themselves a restriction on the supply of the service" (GATS 1994, Art. VI). EU and US-style agreements mirror that same standard while stepping up the binding nature of that standard. The GATS provision acts only as a basis for future rulemaking by the Council for Trade in Services; however, the standard in US and some EU agreements is self-enforcing – the parties must meet those standards or risk violating the agreement (GATS 1994, Art. VI; DR–CAFTA 2004, Art. 11.8; US–Chile 2003, Art. 11.8; US–Singapore 2003, Art. 8.8; EU–Chile 2002, Art. 102; NAFTA 1993, Art. 1210).[35]

Human capital development

The most direct way for countries to improve their services sectors is through local human capital development. Countries have employed numerous means to this end, including opening their borders to migration and immigration and investing heavily in public education. In the case of opening borders, it is the developing countries that favor liberalization over protection, and the developed world that resists. Under the GATS (1994, Art. VI), countries may schedule commitments to remove barriers to migration and immigration. EU-style agreements also allow for such commitments, but in most cases, the EU offers only minimal liberalization of their own borders (for example, EU–Chile 2002, Art. 95; ActionAid et al. 2008). US agreements simply omit border liberalization from the scope of the services provisions, permitting all kinds of restrictions on the free movement of persons (for example, DR–CAFTA 2004, Art. 11.1).

International trade agreements rarely interfere with government investments in public education. Where WTO members recognize the licensing of schools and teachers of another member, those countries must give other members a chance to negotiate recognition of their own licensing procedures (GATS 1994, Art. VII). However, the WTO does not require that countries harmonize their domestic licensing standards or automatically recognize that of other trade partners. Instead, such licensing is subject to the same standard of reasonableness, objectivity and impartiality as all other domestic regulation mentioned in the previous section.[36] The biggest obstacles to public education investments, however, come from the domestic political and economic situation within the developing countries. Where they have no money to invest, or where the money is poorly used or inequitably distributed, countries may not be able to build up their human capital effectively.

Services commitments and South–South complacence

Across the board, international agreements in services trade have limited the policy options available to countries directing public policy toward diversification and growth. Surprisingly, South–South arrangements have done little to either preserve or increase policy space in this area. Services commitments are relatively new in the arena of free trade agreements; they are often negotiated once an agreement on goods is in place. Consequently, many South–South agreements, such as China–Chile and SAFTA, have not yet concluded a section on services, and the CAN (1998, Arts 14–16), under Secretariat Decision 439, contains only minimal services obligations.

MERCOSUR's Montevideo Protocol (1997, Art. IV), by far the most comprehensive South–South services agreement, contains largely GATS-equivalent language, especially as regards market access commitments. As a result, these agreements retain the flexibilities existent under the WTO and GATS but nothing more. Trade in services has come to mean, in addition to cross-border trade and movement of natural persons, the supply of services through commercial presence abroad – also known as foreign direct investment.[37] Although the WTO and EU frameworks treat most investment provisions as services disciplines, the US addresses it in a separate investment chapter that more rigidly constrains the use of domestic measures to control foreign investors as well as foreign capital. The next section discusses the various policy limits on foreign investment regulation imposed by modern trading regimes.

Investment

Countries have historically had at their fingertips numerous creatively crafted investment measures aimed to protect domestic industry, preserve their current and capital account balances, create local backward and forward linkages and otherwise strengthen their economy. These measures address both foreign direct and portfolio investment – that is, both companies and capital. Table 4.7 lays out the current availability of these measures under trade agreement models.

Performance requirements for foreign direct investment

The WTO treats FDI under two different schemes: goods and services. Investment measures related to trade in services are covered under the

Table 4.7. Investment checklist

Policy instrument	WTO and associated agreements	US agreements	EU agreements
Domestic content requirements	X	X	X
Trade balancing requirements	X	X	X
Foreign exchange restrictions	X	X	X
Domestic sales restrictions	X	X	X
Domestic producer preference	X	X	√[38]
Local management requirements	√	X	√
Technology transfer	√	X	√
Local labor requirements	√	X[39]	√
Headquarters/production restrictions	√	X	√
Research and development obligations	√	X	√
Infrastructure provisions	√	√	√
Subsidized credit/entrepreneurship	√	√	√
Administrative guidance	√	√	√
International transfer/payment restrictions	X	X	X

GATS.[40] With respect to investment measures related to trade in goods, the WTO provides a baseline of prohibited measures under two broad WTO principles.

The Agreement on Trade Related Investment Measures (TRIMS) prohibits any measures that violate national treatment (Article III) or the general obligation to eliminate quantitative restrictions (Article XI). It then lays out an illustrative list of prohibited measures in an appended annex (TRIMS 1994). Under TRIMS, countries may not require that foreign investors achieve a certain level of domestic content in their goods or prefer domestic producers or products in their production process. They may not limit foreign investors' imports in relation to their local production or export levels. They may not require investors to acquire foreign exchange only through export, and they may not demand that investors sell a certain amount of their product within the domestic market. Furthermore, WTO members may not create incentives for investors by requiring any of the above as a condition for receiving economic advantages (Correa and Kumar 2003).

EU-style agreements treat FDI as the supply of a service through commercial presence (Mode 3 of the GATS framework). The EU–Chile (2002) agreement contains a separate section entitled "Establishment" that protects the establishment of foreign investors within the territory of a party.[41] EU–CARIFORUM (2008, Arts 67–8, 70) also covers commercial presence separately from other modes of supply, protecting foreign investors from measures violating national treatment, MFN and imposing quantitative restrictions. All this, however, adds virtually nothing to the basic WTO standards already in place.

Modern North–South trading regimes can be divided into two camps: TRIMS and TRIMS+. While the EU generally maintains the TRIMS standard in its trade agreements, the US tacks on several "plus" provisions that put additional limits on government policymakers. In addition to domestic content, trade balancing, foreign exchange, preference for domestic producers and domestic sales obligations, US agreements forbid export level requirements, technology and knowledge transfer demands, local supply exclusivity and management nationality prerequisites (NAFTA 1993, Art. 1106; DR–CAFTA 2004, Art. 10.9; US–Chile 2003, Art. 10.9; US–Singapore 2003, Art. 15.8).

The "plus" provisions in US agreements help to shed light on the policy flexibility available under the TRIMS model. The more permissive model allows countries to impose numerous measures historically applied to promote local development, including requirements to export a certain level or percentage of goods, to transfer technology developed locally, supply exclusively from the territory and hire local management (NAFTA 1993, Arts 1106–7; TRIMS 1994). Of course, these measures remain subject to the pillars of national treatment and MFN treatment under the WTO, as do all measures of WTO member countries (ActionAid et al. 2008). Additionally, the GATS (1994, Art. XIX) permits developing countries to attach some conditions to their services liberalization commitments with development in mind.

Even under TRIMS+ some flexibilities that countries have employed with varying success to promote development. Members of US-style agreements may continue to create incentives for export, technology transfer and backward and forward linkages by providing advantages to companies that comply with certain standards. US treaties also permit countries to condition advantages on compliance with requirements "to locate production, supply a service, train or employ workers, construct or expand particular facilities, or carry out research and development, in its territory" (NAFTA 1993, Art. 1106; DR–CAFTA 2004, Art. 10.9; US–Chile 2003, Art. 10.5; US–Singapore 2003, Art. 15.8).

Certain other measures lay outside of the scope of these investment provisions, making them available to all countries that have the capacity to impose and enforce them. Members of both TRIMS and TRIMS+ agreements may still invest in local infrastructure to promote direct investment. Countries may also provide directed credit in key industries to draw investors into specific sectors and administrative guidance to multinational companies seeking to expand in to local markets.[42]

Capital controls and transfer restrictions

Countries have also attempted to regulate capital flows and other international transfers and payments to promote and stabilize their development. Restrictions on foreign portfolio investment (FPI), however, are generally disfavored within modern trade agreement models. The WTO, EU agreements and US agreements all prohibit international transfer and payment restrictions presumptively (GATS 1994, Art. XI; DR–CAFTA 2004, Arts 10.8, 11.10; NAFTA 1993, Art. 1109; US–Chile 2003, Art. 10.8; US–Singapore 2003, Arts 8.10, 15.7; EU–Chile 2002, Art. 163; EU–Mexico 2001, Art. 29; EU–Tunisia 1998, Art. 33; EU–South Africa 1999, Art. 33).[43] The difference here lies in the exceptions. The WTO employs the positive list approach to bind only those sectors with specific liberalization commitments. The WTO model, mirrored here by most EU agreements, also provides an exception in the case of "serious balance of payments and external financial difficulties," which is the primary purpose for such measures (EU–Chile 2002, Arts 166, 195; EU–Mexico 2001, Arts 30–31; EU–South Africa 1999, Arts 32–34; EU–Tunisia 1998, Art. 35; GATS 1994, Art. XII).

The US model, as well as some recent EU agreements like EU–CARIFORUM, applies the restriction on capital controls across sectors and industries (DR–CAFTA 2004, Art. 10.8; US–Chile 2003, Art. 10.8; US–Singapore 2003, Art. 15.7; NAFTA 1993, Art. 1109; EU–CARIFORUM 2008, Arts 122–24). Foreign capital receives the same treatment as foreign companies here – protection regardless of any specific liberalization commitments. US-style agreements also place one more restraint on policy options by omitting the balance-of-payments exception.

Investor-state arbitration

The US goes one step further, indirectly binding policymakers' hands in introducing investment measures through investor-state arbitration. Unlike the WTO and EU-style agreements, which only make room for dispute resolution between treaty partners, the US allows private investors to sue states for interfering with the value of their investment (for example, EU–CARIFORUM 2008, ch. 2; DSU 1994, sec. B). They rely on general treaty language prohibiting expropriation, discrimination, and unfair or inequitable treatment, which has been interpreted broadly by private arbitral tribunals (Van Harten 2009). NAFTA is the only agreement in force long enough to have a history of investor-state disputes and since then a few agreements have attempted to clarify certain treaty standards (Edsall 2006). However, more recent agreements that contain the same investor-state arbitration provisions do not escape the risk of regulatory chill caused by NAFTA's arbitration history.

South–South investment liberalization and protection

In response to the constraints of the US model investment provision, some developing countries have created South–South trading relationships, like MERCOSUR and CAN, that liberalize investment regionally and protect against foreign investors from without.[44] Both MERCOSUR and CAN echo provisions of North–South agreements. MERCOSUR (1994, Art. 3) incorporates the US model language for national treatment and CAN (1991a, Art. 15) prohibits transfer and payments restrictions. However, they enforce strict ownership requirements on foreign firms in order for them to qualify for protection under the regime. Under CAN, for example, companies must be owned at least 60 percent by national investors of two or more community members. Additionally, for any country whose investor contributes at least 15 percent of the capital for the enterprise, one of the directors must be a national of that country (CAN 1991a, Art. 1(d)–(e)).

These South–South trade agreements provide an example of how to combine substantial investment liberalization with regional protection of nascent industry. The nature of the trading partner makes a difference however, as bargaining and informational asymmetries between developed and developing countries lead to North–South arrangements with the same terms placing undesired constraints on policymakers. Beyond investment protection, one more area of "trade-related" discipline has drawn the attention of international human rights groups and developing nations alike: intellectual property rules.

International intellectual property protection

Historically, countries have employed intellectual property rules in an attempt to balance global integration with domestic development, correcting informational asymmetries while creating financial incentives for inventors and protecting private property. This balance has become particularly contentious when protecting private property leads to limiting access to necessary medicines. Wealthier countries, as knowledge exporters, have prioritized incentives for knowledge creation, while poor countries, as knowledge importers have favored incentives for knowledge dissemination (Shadlen 2005b).

Today, however, the global trade regime places increasing limits on the ability of developing countries to promote such dissemination. International intellectual property rules have come under attack, in part, because of their adverse effect on medicinal availability in the developing world. For that reason, the WTO issued the Declaration on the Trade Related Intellectual Property Rights (TRIPS) Agreement and Public Health (Doha Declaration), which emphasized the importance of developing country concerns about their access to medicines (WTO 2001). Despite the controversy, the US continues to push for stronger inventor incentives at the expense of policy flexibility. Table 4.8 provides a broad picture of the policy constraints over IPRS.

Table 4.8. Intellectual property checklist

Policy instrument	WTO and associated agreements	US agreements	EU agreements
Patent restriction by industry/origin	X	X	X
Limit IP protection for plants/animals	√	X	√+
Permit early working on patented pharmaceuticals	√	X	√
Compulsory licensing	√	√+	√
Local production requirement	√	X	√
Parallel imports	√	X	√+
Limiting patent breadth	√	√	√
Utility models	√	√	√

Patent restriction by industry, origin or duration

The most direct way of intervening in the delicate balance between information dissemination and information protection is by controlling the industries, origins and duration of patent terms. In this one question, these three trade agreement models concur. Patent restriction by industry, origin or duration is patently (no pun intended) prohibited under the agreement on TRIPS of the WTO. TRIPS (Art. 27.1) states that "patents shall be available for *any* inventions, whether products or processes, *in all fields of technology*, provided that they are new, involve an inventive step and are capable of industrial application." This language is echoed in all US trade agreements and likewise incorporated into most EU agreements by reference (NAFTA 1993,

Art. 1709; DR–CAFTA 2004, Art. 15.9; US–Chile 2003, Art. 17.9; US–Singapore 2003, Art. 16.7; EU–Mexico 2001, Art. 36(1)(a); EU–Chile 2002, Art. 170(a)(i); EU–South Africa 1999, Art. 46). TRIPS (Art. 33) also requires that all patents last 20 years, minimum, a duration limit adopted by both EU and US agreements (for example, NAFTA 1993, Art. 1709).[45]

Limited plant and animal protection

For countries where populations rely heavily on traditional knowledge of plants and animals, limiting protection of such intellectual property ensures that the people will continue to have needed access to food and medicines. Although plant and animal species are generally found in nature (and therefore not new or innovative), the US and other developed countries have sought intellectual property protection for genetically modified plant species – a move that places access of native populations to their traditional knowledge in jeopardy. All international IPR regimes demand some protection over knowledge derived from plant and animal life. TRIPS allows countries to exclude plants and animals from patentability, with the exception of microorganisms, but requires that some effective protection for plant varieties be put into place (TRIPS 1994, Art. 27). This requirement admits some theoretical flexibility for WTO members to establish their own plant variety protection systems – a flexibility that many countries have exploited (Shadlen 2005b).

Bilateral North–South trade models have tightened that flexibility down, specifying a minimum type of plant variety protection required to comply with the agreement. EU agreements, for example, often require trade partners who have not yet acceded to the International Convention for the Protection of New Varieties of Plants (UPOV), either from 1978 or 1991,[46] do so within a reasonable time from entry into force and US agreements generally require accession to the latter (DR–CAFTA 2004, Art. 15.1; US–Chile 2003, Art. 17.1; US–Singapore 2003, Art. 16.1).[47] The US model also demands that contracting states "make every effort" to impose a plant patenting system. US–Singapore even omits the TRIPS flexibility of excluding plants from the patent system. (DR–CAFTA 2004, Art. 15.9; US–Chile 2003, Art. 17.9; US–Singapore 2003, Art. 16.7).

Information disclosure and "Bolar" provisions

Some countries promote knowledge dissemination by establishing strict information disclosure requirements. They then make the information available to generics producers and domestic inventors who want to piggyback off the patented invention or begin working on generic equivalents before the patent term ends. The TRIPS model requires that patent applicants disclose the information necessary "for the invention to be carried out by a person skilled in the art." It also allows members to demand that applicants "indicate the best mode for carrying out the invention known to the inventor at the filing date." Even on unpatented products, countries often require applicants to submit additional data for regulatory approval (TRIPS 1994, Art. 29).

Early working or "Bolar" provisions build on these disclosure requirements, permitting producers to develop, test and begin the registration process for generic versions of patented pharmaceuticals before the end of the patent term (Shadlen 2005b). Although the text of TRIPS only proscribes "unfair commercial use" of protected data, WTO case law reveals that TRIPS permits early working so long as it does not result in commercial production or stockpiling purposes (TRIPS 1994, Art. 39).[48]

While EU agreements are modeled after the TRIPS standards, the US model favors knowledge creation and protection. US agreements do not allow more than minimum disclosure requirements and they protect data submitted for regulatory approval for at least five years "against both disclosure and reliance" (for example, DR–CAFTA 2004, Art. 15.10; Shadlen 2005b, 19).

Compulsory licensing

In order to gain access to patented drugs and necessary technology in the absence of a traditionally negotiated license, governments have granted compulsory licenses (CLs) to domestic industry to make and distribute those products (Shadlen 2005b). TRIPS establishes the internationally accepted procedural standard for CLs, implicitly adopted by both EU and US trade agreements. TRIPS Article 31 requires that countries consider each license individually, that they attempt to negotiate a license from the patent holder "on reasonable commercial terms" over a reasonable period of time (except in situations of national emergency), that they limit the scope and duration of the license to a specific purpose, that they grant a nonexclusive and nonassignable license, that they grant it only for the domestic market and that they subject it to judicial review, among other procedural requirements.

Countries have also used CLs in order to encourage local production of patented products. Brazil, for example, allows the government to grant CLs to local producers when a patented good is not produced locally within three years from the beginning of the patent term. This promotes "the transfer of non-codified, tacit knowledge that occurs via the localization of manufacturing operations" (Shadlen 2005, 22). Although these measures have been somewhat controversial, no WTO ruling has outlawed them and they remain available under TRIPS.

Some US agreements have circumscribed the use of CLs beyond the procedural requirements of Article 31 and definitively prohibited such local production requirements (for example, US–Chile 2003, Art. 17.9).[49] US–Singapore (Art. 16.7), for example, only allows CLs to remedy anticompetitive practices, for public noncommercial use or in the case of national emergency. Furthermore, patent term marketing restrictions in agreements such as DR–CAFTA (Art. 15.10) may create an effective ban on compulsory licensing (Abbott 2004).

US–Peru, on the other hand, incorporates the 2003 Doha Declaration on Public Health, recommitting to Article 31 which emphasizes that countries may establish their own grounds for providing CLs and allows countries to grant these licenses for export to least developed countries and to countries without production capacity (WTO 2001). The US–Peru (2006) agreement may be evidence of international pressure to improve access to medicines for the poorest populations, and indicate that even bilateral agreements cannot place too many limits on policy space in this area (Shadlen 2005b).

Patent exhaustion

As an indirect route to promoting access to needed technologies, countries may establish their own exhaustion policies under TRIPS (Art. 6) – whether national, regional or international – implicitly permitting parallel imports of goods where the patent holder's rights have been exhausted. Where international exhaustion policies apply, a producer from a developing country could purchase goods from an industrialized country producer, repackage the goods and undersell the industrialized producer in a third country. Developing countries can use this advantage to increase competition and drive down prices, making patented products more affordable (Shadlen 2005b).

Since exhaustion is a matter of domestic policy, few trade agreements have addressed the issue. The US applies a national standard of exhaustion which allows patent holders to assert their patent rights against all parallel imports, regardless of their origin. Within the European Community, countries apply a regional exhaustion policy which protects against parallel imports from outside the union (Strauss 2001). A few US agreements, however, have attempted to export the national standard to treaty partners. US FTAs with Morocco and Australia both demand that the countries recognize national exhaustion of patent rights (US–Morocco 2004, 17.9; US–Australia 2004, 15.9). Although EU agreements have not, thus far, exported their exhaustion policies to their trade partners, regional exhaustion will restrict producers originating outside the union from competing with EU patent holders by way of parallel imports.

Patent alternatives

Unlike the above aspects of patent protection, countries retain flexibility in limiting patent breadth and protecting otherwise unpatentable inventions through "utility models" (Shadlen 2005b, 15–16). The latter measures, in particular, provide local residents with room for creative expansion on existing patents and incentives for their own experimentation.

Neither the more permissive WTO model nor US-style agreements address patent breadth or utility models directly. Some EU agreements, however, expressly allow utility models "provided that they are new, involve some degree of nonobviousness and are capable of industrial application" (EU–CARIFORUM 2008, Art. 148). Although it is not clear whether such a provision would increase the use of utility models by mentioning them, or further tie the hands of policymakers by limiting the conditions under which they are granted, it at least shows promise that the developed world recognizes other types of invention incentives.

South–South responses and the US model

For developing countries, intellectual property rights represents a new area of trade-related issues that has yet to be addressed under most South–South agreements. The Andean Community, however, has established a model South–South arrangement that includes intellectual property provisions aimed at promoting the interests of the nations in that region. First of all, the CAN (2000, Art. 3) demands that patent applications based on material obtained from traditional knowledge meet the requirements of international law, the Andean Community and domestic law with respect to acquisition of that material. In addition, the community excludes scientific theories, mathematical methods and living things (whatever the size), among other pursuits, from patentability (Art. 15).

Like many developing countries, the decisions of the CAN Secretariat apply an international standard for exhaustion, making room for the benefits provided by parallel imports (CAN 2000, Art. 54; Musungu et al. 2004). Also similar to Brazil's intellectual property law (see above), the CAN (Arts 61, 65–6) allows compulsory licensing when the patent holder does not exploit the patent locally within three years of the grant of that patent. Finally, the decision explicitly mentions utility models, which can encourage a lower degree of innovation often "more appropriate for local firms" (CAN 2000, Arts 81–5; Shadlen 2005b, 16).

The Andean Community model for South–South intellectual property protection demonstrates how developing countries can work together to encourage information dissemination and establish financial incentives for creativity. Unfortunately, as countries seek trade agreements with both the Global North and Global South, the CAN model has come into conflict with the more restrictive US agreement model.

The US–Peru Trade Promotion Agreement (a comprehensive FTA) entered into force in January of 2009. As a condition of the agreement, Peru must undertake "reasonable efforts" to establish a plant patenting system – a measure that is forbidden under the Andean Community intellectual property regime. The CAN Commission met multiple times to consider this and other conflicts between the agreements and it concluded that Peru (and the other Andean nations) may "develop and deepen" intellectual property protection through trade agreements with the US (Ramírez 2008). If this trend continues, then the flexibilities exploited in South–South regional integration will be short-lived and the US model may become the *de facto* standard for intellectual property protection.

Summary and Conclusions

This chapter shows that the current global trade regime substantially curtails the ability of countries to maintain control over various policy tools that traditionally have been deployed as part of long-run development paths.[50] Still, under the WTO, despite the constraint on policy space, there remains considerable room to maneuver. Countries may, legally, raise and lower tariffs, provide tax-related export incentives such as drawbacks and deferrals within EPZs, impose certain performance requirements on investors and service providers and employ domestic patent laws to prioritize information dissemination over incentives for invention. The WTO also makes extra room for developing countries to form bilateral and regional trade agreements under the Enabling Clause (GATT 1979).

Despite wide variation among bilateral and regional agreements, policy space under North–South free trade agreements are the most constraining on the traditional industrial development toolkit. Overwhelmingly, among both bilateral agreements and the multilateral trade regime, the trend heads toward demanding increased liberalization and decreased government intervention in the economy. At the same time, some types of agreements continue to make space for the policies aimed at industrial development, while others push for broader and deeper liberalization. As shown above, trade agreements with the EU retain much of the flexibility under the WTO in the areas of investment and intellectual property, and employ the same positive-list approach as the global regime when it comes to services trade. By contrast, the US imposes many additional disciplines on its trading partners – expanding patent protection, mandating investment liberalization and employing a negative-list approach to services bindings. Since the early 1990s, trade regimes have formed around these principles and US trade policy has become more uniform. Meanwhile, EU trade policy varies by trading partner, indicating a greater willingness to permit certain policies in these areas. Provided this trend continues, countries that are still developing in 30 years will have more opportunity to creatively use their policy space under an EU agreement than under an agreement with the US.

Many South–South agreements are still formally notified to the WTO under Article XXIV; yet they often provide the greatest policy space among the agreements we studied. This flexibility derives not from lacking affirmative trade disciplines but from using trade liberalization between developing countries to protect industries and promote growth regionally. Investment and intellectual property rules under the CAN provide the clearest example here. The CAN rules of origin establish protection for regional firms against extra-regional companies. In addition, the CAN explicitly protects traditional knowledge, tightens patentability requirements and makes room for local, nonpatentable innovation.

Still, some policy space remains under even the most restrictive trading schemes. To the extent the state is economically capable, a country may invest heavily in public education, subsidize credit to certain industries and build up domestic infrastructure. A method employed by developing and developed countries alike, policymakers may also provide administrative guidance – marketing the country, its location, natural resources and workforce, for example – to investors and traders internationally. This technique may help a country to target an industry that would transfer technology or provide backward and forward linkages in the economy.

Notes

1 Pecuniary externalities affect third parties through price fluctuations but not necessarily through the misallocation of resources.

2 Although countries have used various controls over government procurement to promote local industry, those measures, for purposes of space and time, remain outside the scope of this chapter.

3 As a caveat before going forward, the agreements within each trade regime are by no means homogenous. Within each of the principal trade areas, the regimes contain some measure of variation. This chapter attempts to draw some generalizations about disciplines under each trade regime. Where the agreements significantly depart from each other, however, the difference is noted.

4 As with all measures under the WTO, even permitted policies are subject to the two pillars of the WTO: nondiscrimination and national treatment (GATT 1947, Arts I, III).

5 These South–South arrangements are by far the least uniform. Thus, the designations in this column represent generalizations from the later analysis.

6 This and other policies may be permitted despite violating certain WTO rules if they pass as legitimate public welfare regulations (GATT 1994, Art. 63).

7 For example, note the many trade related issues covered under MERCOSUR (trade in goods and services, intellectual property rights, investment and safeguards) and CAN (goods, services, intellectual property, and intra- and extra-regional investments) (MERCOSUR 1991a, 1991b, 1994, 1995, 1997; CAN 1991a, 1991b, 1998, 2000, 2003).

8 The degree of procedural requirements varies greatly between agreements (EU–Chile 2002, Arts 92, 195; EU–Mexico 2000, Arts 15, 21).

9 Among US and EU disciplines, the rules are not identical across agreements.

10 Take, for example, Chile's tariff profile as provided by the WTO. While the simple average bound is 25.1 percent, the simple average applied is much lower at 6 percent. This trend repeats for the countries in this study (WTO 2010b; WTO 2012a).

11 This trend repeats itself over and over again in the countries' individual tariff schedules. Taking a simple average of the bound rates under the RTAs and comparing it to the simple average of the MFN applied rate across all products would prove this conclusively. Unfortunately, we were unable to find a schedules document that would export to a spreadsheet program and take such averages.

12 This represents a bound tariff after progressive reduction over seven years (NAFTA 1993).

13 The WTO also treats import licenses as quotas, and has a separate annex governing the use of licenses in cases where they are permitted (ILP 1994).

14 DR–CAFTA also expressly incorporates the WTO Agreement on Import Licensing, and imposes an additional notification requirement (Art. 3.9). However, neither NAFTA, US–Singapore, US–Peru, nor US–Colombia have any exceptions for balance-of-payments difficulties or shortages.

15 Export incentives based on geography are often called export processing zones (EPZs) (ILO 2008).

16 Mexico's *maquiladora* program provides a ready example of such a system. Under NAFTA, however, "*maquila* firms were granted a seven-year phase-in period during which they continued to enjoy duty-free importation benefits." This ended in January 2001, when NAFTA article 303 entered into effect (Sargent and Matthews 2001).

17 Several EU-style treaties prohibit the use of taxation to protect domestic industry, which could indirectly restrict tax-based export incentives (EU–Chile 2002, Art. 63; EU–Mexico 2000, Art. 13; EU–CARIFORUM 2008, Art. 13). By contrast, EU agreements with several African nations implicitly permit drawbacks by limiting the amount to that of the original tax (EU–Tunisia 1998, Art. 22; EU–South Africa 1999, Art. 21). This provision seems to be aimed at preventing hidden export subsidies – payments called "drawbacks" or "deferrals" by the government, but which actually exceed the amount of the tax.

18 The one exception here is US–Singapore.

19 This does not include conditions, however, that the good be subsequently exported and other such rules as required under NAFTA (US–Chile 2003, Art. 3.24; DR–CAFTA 2004, Art. 3.31).

20 EU–Tunisia, however, excludes express safeguards for balance of payments (Arts 25–6), while EU–South Africa makes no allowance for goods trade safeguards for balance of payments or shortages (Arts 24, 26). EU–CARIFORUM likewise makes no room for safeguards in the case of shortages (Arts 25, 240).

21 Since the agreements mention nothing about shortages, safeguards to protect against them are presumed prohibited.

22 The only US agreement to take special consideration of developing countries, DR–CAFTA Article 8.1(4), places limitations on imposing safeguards against developing countries.

23 Both the South Asia Free Trade Agreement (SAFTA) and the Southern Cone Common Market (MERCOSUR) contain "sensitive lists" within the agreement, and SAFTA even permits countries to maintain NTBs on such sensitive products (SAFTA 2004, Arts 7.3 and 7.5; MERCOSUR 1991a, Art. 6).

24 Article 101 of the China–Chile Agreement, for example, exempts all tax issues from coverage by the agreement (China–Chile 2005).

25 While some amount of control is permitted under all agreements, US agreements employ a negative list rather than the positive list approach of the GATS and EU agreements.

26 Here, the EU agreements could be evolving to look more like US agreements but the rules are not consistent across the four treaties.

27 The difference here is that the balancing test for regulations is self-enforcing under the EU and US agreements, while enforcement under the WTO requires further rulemaking.

28 It is important to note, however, that the WTO contains inherently the expectation of full liberalization across sectors eventually (GATS 1994).

29 Although the four EU agreements studied here contain actual services commitments only to varying degrees, each contains a reference to the positive list approach stated in their negotiating mandate at the very least. And like the WTO, with the exception of EU–Tunisia, these agreements call for the eventual elimination of "substantially all remaining discrimination between the parties" in all sectors and all modes of supply (EU–Mexico 2001, Art. 7; EU–Chile 2002, Art. 100; EU–South Africa 1999, Art. 30.1).

30 The exception to many of these rules is NAFTA, since it came about so much earlier – on this subject it states: "The Parties shall periodically, but in any event at least every two years, endeavor to negotiate the liberalization or removal of the quantitative restrictions set out in Annex V pursuant to paragraphs 1 through 3" (NAFTA 1993, Art. 1207.4).

31 Restricting foreign capital participation may also be prohibited through maintaining the right of establishment, present in all US agreements and discussed below.

32 Also known as the "right of non-establishment."

33 The agreement also indirectly refers to "establishment" in Article 224 on General Exceptions, however, the context would indicate that the word means "direct investment" rather than any general right of establishment (EU–CARIFORUM 2008, Art. 224(1)).

34 One author mentions that while the US agreements contain clearer language about the prohibition of duty of establishment clauses, they may not necessarily be "more forceful in actually putting them into effect" (Marconini 2006, 9).

35 By contrast, EU–Mexico (2001, Art. 8) contains only a vague "regulatory carve out" for parties wishing to regulate services supply. The EU–South Africa and EU–Tunisia agreements also have only a skeletal services section, which acts as more of an agreement to agree than a commitment to liberalize services immediately.

36 Consequently, as mentioned above, EU and US agreements maintain the same standard for such licensing, with potentially stronger enforcement abilities.

37 Designated under the GATS framework as Mode 3 (GATS 1994, Art. 1).

38 In EU agreements, these measures may be effectively proscribed by other rules.

39 For local labor requirements, local management requirements, headquarters restrictions, technology transfer and research and development, a country may not require them as a condition of entry, but may condition receipt of a benefit on them.

40 Since the policy flexibilities and constraints of the GATS are discussed earlier, this section focuses on WTO treatment of investment measures related to trade in goods.

41 While the other EU agreements incorporate sections entitled "Services and Establishment," as mentioned above, they are largely agreements to agree in the future rather than active commitments between the parties.

42 The test for domestic regulation is articulated in full in Section C.4.

43 It should be noted that under the EU agreements, Chile reserved a hefty exception for their investment law 600, and Mexico retains an exception for exchange and monetary difficulties in addition to balance of payments.

44 For example, the MERCOSUR Protocol on Investment Promotion and Protection contains the same national treatment standard as that provided under US agreements (MERCOSUR 1994, Art. 3). Likewise. CAN Decision 292 allows multinational enterprises the right to establish subsidiaries, transfer payments freely, and transfer their domicile freely (CAN 1991a, Art. 15).

45 This minimum is not even mentioned in DR–CAFTA, US–Chile or US–Singapore, but is implied. The minimum is likewise not mentioned explicitly in EU trade agreements.

46 The key difference between the 1978 and 1991 conventions is found in their allowance of third parties "to use protected seeds and plants for breeding new varieties." UPOV 1978 included a farmers exception allowing them to reuse seeds. This exception was eliminated under UPOV 1991, "which provides much stronger rights to breeders" (Shadlen 2005b, 13).

47 NAFTA, largely because of when it was negotiated and signed, required only the UPOV 1978 (Art. 1701.2).

48 This standard has been determined by WTO case law and is not necessarily clear from the text of the agreement.

49 Once more, the early conclusion of NAFTA resulted in a substantially different intellectual property rights regime. Since the conclusion of NAFTA, the US model has evolved and moved further away from the more flexible disciplines in TRIPS.

50 Part of the reasons for this is that, with the spread of globalization, no issue is truly "uniquely" domestic. Even though industry standards, licensures, and certifications may be matters of domestic law, they impact foreign companies and, by extension, foreign governments.

Chapter 5

UNDERSTANDING DEVELOPING COUNTRY RESISTANCE TO THE DOHA ROUND

Nowhere has the clash of globalizations become more acute than in the Doha Round negotiations at the WTO. Development concerns were enshrined in the round during its inception and have been the core of controversy ever since. Indeed, lack of agreement on development has been the core reason why the round has now collapsed three times since 2001: in Cancun 2003, Hong Kong 2005 and Geneva 2008.

Talks collapsed around a convergence of two things. First, the market access benefits to the developing (and developed) world were shrinking and small. Second, the developing world saw real costs in terms of the shrinking of policy space for successful globalization, especially as it became more and more clear that developed countries were not willing to yield on even those measures (agriculture concessions) that would bring the small gains. Unlike the Uruguay Round, the developing countries were not willing to trade away development sovereignty for small economic gains for the few.

The fact that there was a development mandate to begin with, and that developing countries have managed to reject proposals by rich countries that would hinder their ability to manage globalization for national development, is new. This is largely due to new market power exhibited by those developing countries that have been the most successful globalizers since the end of the Uruguay Round: China, India, Brazil, South Africa and the numerous countries that formed strong coalitions with them.

This chapter has four parts that chronicle the clash of globalizations under the Doha Round. A short first part discusses the establishment of the round, part two examines the Cancun Ministerial in 2003, part three the Hong Kong Ministerial in 2005, and the fourth part evaluates the July 2008 "mini-ministerial" in Geneva and beyond.

A WTO Round Centered on Development

In 1999 the world's trade ministers gathered in Seattle, USA for a ministerial that some hoped would launch a new round of global trade negotiations. Indeed, since they were to be launched in the US there was a buzz about them being the "Clinton Round." We all know what happened in Seattle. Major conflict arose inside and outside the talks, and they collapsed. Outside, which grabbed the headlines and is now the subject of a major motion picture titled *The Battle of Seattle*, tens of thousands of protestors from all walks of life converged. Environmentalists dressed as turtles protested that the WTO was hurting national environmental laws, trade unionists marched for job security and wages in a globalizing world, social justice advocates from across the globe protested what they saw as violations in the WTO of human rights, access to public health and democracy. Inside, there was a rift between developed and developing countries, a clash of globalizations.

Developing countries argued that a new round should only take place after a full evaluation of the Uruguay Round was conducted. In hindsight, the Uruguay Round wasn't a grand bargain after all. According to Faizel Ismail, the head of South Africa's delegation to the WTO:

> Developing Countries felt that the Uruguay Round Agreements were unfair as not only did they fail to provide equitable access for the products of developing country markets, but they also created greater burdens upon developing countries and eroded their policy space.[1]

More specifically, they felt that the developed countries did not live up to their part of the Uruguay Round (UR) bargain in terms of market access. What's more, they felt that many of the WTO agreements were cutting into their ability to deploy effective development strategies. Among the most egregious violations of the UR to development sovereignty in the developing world was the TRIPS, which turned out to make medicines and other products more expensive and constrain the ability of nations to engage in the innovation and industrial upgrading policies enjoyed by rich countries in previous decades. The TRIMS was also of grave concern because it outlawed measures like local content standards. Finally, the Agreement on Agriculture allowed the developed countries to maintain their high protection through high domestic support and tariffs while requiring the developing countries to liberalise their food imports, at levels that were seen as detrimental to food security and farmers' livelihoods.

In Seattle, developed countries wanted to rush on and negotiate new agreements on the internet, deepen TRIPS and TRIMS and perhaps even negotiate a "Social Clause" which would set global labor standards in the WTO. What's more, such an agenda was to be negotiated in "green room" negotiating sessions where most developing countries would be left out. One group wanted to rush ahead, the other wanted to adjust the past. These two positions clashed and everyone went home.

September 11th 2001 is said to have changed everything, and the WTO is no exception. In an act of unity for a more peaceful world, developing countries agreed to a ministerial in Doha, Qatar in November 2001. During that ministerial the developing countries agreed to pursue a new round as long as development was the core theme and mandate for the round's outcome. Such an act of unity set the stage for the current clash of globalizations.

To the developing countries, a development round (referred to herein as the Doha Development Round (DDR)) meant:

> A fairer trading system that would allow products from developing countries greater access to developed country markets; a review of the rules of the WTO that have shrunk the policy space of developing countries when developed countries have used these same policy tools for their own development in previous decades, providing capacity to developing countries to implement new rules and build their supply-side capacity and to participate meaningfully in the WTO rule-making system.[2]

One of the core concepts enshrined in the declaration was a mandate for "less than full reciprocity," meaning that developing countries would not have to liberalize more than, or even as much as, developed countries. With these marching orders negotiators entered into a series of negotiations just as broad, if not broader, than the Uruguay Round. The Doha Declaration crafted at the ministerial set out negotiations for IP, investment, competition policy, government procurement, trade facilitation, industrial tariffs and services. The goal for the completion of the round was December of 2004 with a ministerial held on the round's progress slated for Cancun, Mexico in September 2003.

Shrinking Agendas: Cancun, Stage for Another Grand Bargain?

The Cancun meetings of 2003 had promise. New World Bank projections of the benefits of the round were fairly enormous and developed countries had recently agreed to amend the TRIPs agreement to make it easier for poor countries to get access to medicines during medical crises – thereby showing the promise of benefits from market access and the return of some of the policy space lost in the UR. Developed countries thus hoped that there would be the means for another grand bargain – market access to the developed countries' agricultural markets in return for new concessions on "Singapore Issues" (referring to issues tabled at meetings years before in Singapore), TRIPS, TRIMS, government procurement, competition policy, trade facilitation, industrial tariffs and services.

At the 2003 Cancun Ministerial meeting of the WTO, Eveline Herfkens, former World Bank executive director and then executive coordinator for the United Nations' Millennium Development Goals, asserted: "A pro-poor Doha Round could increase global income by as much as $520 billion and lift an additional 144 million people out of poverty. This is why so many hundreds of us come together today."[1] Herfkens was citing World Bank estimates of the gains from full global trade liberalization under the round (see Table 5.2). The bank put the benefits of an ambitious round at $832 billion, $539 billion of which was there for the developing world (okay, so Herfkens was off by $12 billion, but not an order of magnitude!). The majority of those gains came from agricultural liberalization.

In Cancun the US and EU – the two largest protectors of agricultural markets – banded together and submitted a joint text regarding their commitments on agricultural liberalization. Neither the US nor EU wanted to give the other an advantage in agricultural production, so they negotiated together first. The EU and to a certain extent the US also tabled a schedule to move ahead on the so called "Singapore Issues."

Disappointment in the US–EU proposal gave rise to the G-20 (Group of Twenty) led by Brazil, India, South Africa, Argentina, China and others. The G-20 is a group of developing countries established on 20 August 2003 (see list below). Its focus is on agriculture, the central issue of the Doha Development Agenda.

1. Argentina	8. Guatemala	15. Philippines
2. Bolivia	9. India	16. South Africa
3. Brazil	10. Indonesia	17. Tanzania
4. Chile	11. Mexico	18. Thailand
5. China	12. Nigeria	19. Uruguay
6. Cuba	13. Pakistan	20. Venezuela
7. Egypt	14. Paraguay	21. Zimbabwe

The chair of the negotiations in Cancun submitted a text for agreement that included modest cuts to Northern agriculture support in return for movement on the Singapore Issues as well as nonagricultural market access (manufacturing tariffs NAMA) and services liberalization. This was a deal breaker.

The G-20 did not see the agricultural cuts as ample enough for development. What's more, they expanded their reach by working with a group of developing countries that were net food importers. G-20 nations are the big exporting nations, but forged a set of demand that not only included market access in the North but also favored policy space for net food importers. Net food importers wanted protection for "special products" that were key for food security and particularly vulnerable in an integrated world economy. These nations also wanted "special safeguard mechanisms" that would allow nations to raise import tariffs in emergencies where cheap imports flooded domestic markets and swamped out small scale agricultural producers at home.

Moreover, the G-20 and other developing countries saw the deepening of commitments over Singapore Issues as a severe curtailment of policy space. Indeed, in a comprehensive review of the Cancun negotiations based on personal in-depth interviews with the key players involved, Amrita Narlikar and Diana Tussie (2004) state that it was the Singapore Issues that formed the real deal-breaker. They credit the strategies of the coalition as holding on to the development issue at the talks. The coalition overcame many internal challenges, as well as outside pressures. Indeed, the United States reportedly threatened many members by arguing that they would revoke preference schemes or slow regional integration talks with certain members in Latin America (Narklikar and Tussie 2004).

Scorned as a disaster in the North, developing countries saw the outcome of the Cancun Ministerial as a victory, though a bittersweet one. Almost all previous GATT rounds had resulted in developing countries having little say in the outcome of negotiation (Narlikar 2004). So, being able to push back is a major victory alone. What's more, developing countries had secured some of the policy space lost in the UR through the TRIPS amendment, and were able to push back on proposals that would have further shrunk their development sovereignty with respect to investment, competition policy and the like. However, these nations did want market access to the North and did see the WTO as the right venue for such a discussion.

Hong Kong and beyond: Shrinking gains and real costs

Two things have plagued the negotiations since Cancun. First, the amount of gains for developing countries projected for market access had shrunk considerably. Moreover, projected gains were skewed toward the developed world, not the developing countries. Second, proposals by the developed countries in terms of developing country liberalization in manufactures and services industries were seen as shrinking the policy space for effective development policy. Developing countries' new economic power and crafty use of coalitions has enabled them to hold the negotiations at a standstill until these asymmetries are addressed.

Shrinking gains

The WTO reconvened with a ministerial in Hong Kong in 2005, where it took one step forward, two steps backward on the development question. No agreement was reached. Although a recommitment to development ensued in Hong Kong, new projections showed that the benefits for developing countries in terms of market access would be small and skewed toward the North. Moreover, the proposals by developed countries that unfolded in Hong Kong posed real costs in terms of lost policy space.

Most estimates of the gains from trade come from computable general equilibrium (CGE) models. CGE models, resting on prevailing economic theory and numerous simplifying assumptions, attempt to present a quantitative picture, at one point in time, of the full interaction of markets and industries throughout the economy. CGE models not only provide estimates regarding the expansion and contraction of exports and imports; they also project how such changes will affect the supply chains of intermediate goods producers. Moreover, CGE models estimate the endpoint of the subsequent rounds of equilibrating changes, as markets readjust to changing conditions, prices rise and fall, and labor and other resources move from contracting to expanding industries.

A CGE model essentially consists of a series of equations, combined with massive collections of data, representing these complex sectoral relationships within the economy. To generate estimates from the model, these equations are solved twice: once for a recent base year for which data is available, without the new trade policy, and then again for the same year, but with the trade policy change. The difference between the two sets of estimates – for example, the increase or decrease in each industry's output and employment – is taken to represent the effects of the trade policy. Note that the estimates represent hypothetical changes in the economy for a base year in the recent past, holding all other aspects of the economy, and time, constant. Estimates generated from these models represent a one-time increase in the level of a nation's income. For instance, if a CGE model calculates that the benefits to Brazil would amount to 1.8 percent, that means a one-time increase in the level of Brazil's income by 1.8 percent (as opposed to an annual growth rate).

Such models are far from perfect. Indeed, they are often criticized for their unrealistic assumptions. CGE models, among other things, assume perfect competition among all buyers and sellers, fixed technology, employment and fiscal balances, and no externalities (positive or negative). What's more, they only model goods trade. Most trade deals – from the global to bilateral level – involve much more than trade. Sometimes the most sought after and contentious issues of negotiation are now over foreign investment, intellectual property, government procurement, subsidies and services (for a critical assessment of these models see Ackerman and Gallagher 2008). Nevertheless they are considered state of the art and, for better or worse, have become the reference points for quantitative discussions regarding the costs and benefits of world trade.

On the eve of the negotiations, the World Bank produced estimates of the gains from the round that put the potential welfare gains at $287 billion in the year 2015 – just one-third of their level two years before. Projections of gains for developing countries dropped to $90 billion – 0.8 percent of GDP – a reduction of 83 percent, while developing countries' share of global gains has fallen from 60 percent to just 31 percent.[2] This was, of course, of grave concern given that the current negotiations were billed as the "development round" of global trade talks.[3]

Perhaps more alarming is that these estimates presumed a scenario of "full" global trade liberalization. In other words, the models assume that all tariffs and non-tariff trade barriers are completely eliminated in the world economy, a highly unlikely scenario for the current round. To reflect with greater accuratey the more probable results of the present negotiations, the new reports include projections for a "likely Doha scenario" of partial liberalization. The "likely" scenario, according to these models, involves agricultural tariff rate reductions in developed countries of 45, 70 and 75 percent within three bands of existing tariffs, and reductions in developing countries of 35, 40, 50 and 60 percent within four bands of tariffs. The least developed countries are not required to make any reductions in agricultural tariffs. For nonagricultural tariff bindings the scenario calls for 50 percent cuts in developed countries, 33 percent in developing countries and zero in the least developed countries.

The "likely" Doha benefits that the models predict are exhibited in Table 5.1. Under this scenario, global gains for 2015 are just $96 billion, with only $16 billion going to the developing world. The developing country benefits are 0.16 percent of GDP. In terms of per capita, that amounts to $3.13, or less than a penny per day per capita for those living in developing countries. Although most of the attention in the negotiations has been focused on agriculture, developing country gains from "likely" agricultural reforms amount to less than 0.1 percent of GDP – just $9 billion. Likely gains from Northern subsidy reduction are projected at barely $1 billion.[4]

Of the benefits that would flow to developing countries, only a few countries receive those benefits. Half of all the benefits to developing countries are expected to flow to just eight countries: Argentina, Brazil (which stands to receive 23 percent of the developing country benefit), China, India, Mexico, Thailand, Turkey and Vietnam.[5] The World Bank estimates find that regions such as the Middle East and North Africa, and countries such as Mexico and Bangladesh would be worse off (this has been confirmed by all the major estimates on the DDR, see Bouet 2006).

Table 5.1. Benefits of "likely" Doha Round scenario

	Beneficiary region		
	High-income	Developing	World
Total amounts, billions of dollars	80	16	96
Per capita, dollars per person	$79.04	$3.13	$15.67
Percentage of GDP	0.24%	0.16%	0.23%

Another major area of negotiation in the Doha Round is services negotiations. Services trade has been growing faster than goods trade since the 1980s. Developed countries have been pushing developing countries to open up their services markets – especially in the financial and telecommunications sectors – in exchange for market access in agriculture. The World Bank also put together models for services trade benefits but ended up deeming them too "highly speculative" to publish in their Doha Round publications.[6] Not only is trade in services difficult to quantify, but the benefits of removing trade barriers have to be extrapolated for modeling purposes, since "tariffs" in the sector do not exist. "Barriers" to cross-border exchange reside more in the form of domestic investment rules and restrictions on entry into markets in a nation's service sector. Though modeling services trade is considered to be in its infancy and should be interpreted with caution, the estimated benefits of services liberalization are presented in Table 5.2.

Table 5.2. Benefits of services trade liberalization

	(US billions)		
	Total benefits	Per capita	Per GDP
Full liberalization			
World	53.053	9.237	0.002
Developed	34.772	35.704	0.002
Developing	18.281	3.833	0.003
Partial liberalization			
World	23.527	4.096	0.001
Developed	16.607	17.052	0.001
Developing	6.92	1.451	0.001

Like the estimates in goods trade, services trade liberalization is expected to yield relatively small benefits – the majority of which would go to developed countries. Under a full liberalization scenario, the total benefit for the world would be $53 billion. Only 34 percent of those benefits would go to the developing world, amounting to a one-time increase of 0.31 percent of GDP, or a penny per day per capita. The authors' likely scenario of partial liberalization – 50 percent reduction in services trade barriers – would yield only $6.9 billion for the developing world, or 29 percent of the total benefits, which amount to much less than a penny per day for one year. In both scenarios, India, South Africa and China are set to receive more than half the total benefits for developing countries. It should be noted, however, that contrary to goods liberalization, developing countries stand to benefit more from services liberalization as a proportion of GDP, though in both cases the total benefits are much less than 1 percent.[7] Adding the liberalization of goods and services trade together, the total benefits for developing countries amounts to $123.5 billion under full liberalization – 1.1 percent of GDP – and $28.7 billion under a more conservative and more likely Doha scenario. Goods and services trade combined, a likely deal would bring a one-time increase of 0.28 percent in the level of global GDP in 2015.[8]

The World Bank created extensions for their models in order to estimate the extent to which the current round will lift the world's poor over global poverty lines. Like projected welfare gains, the poverty projections are now smaller. The Cancun projection cited by Herfkens of 144 million people who would have theoretically risen out of poverty has now been revised downward to 66 million under the complete liberalization scenario. The "likely" Doha scenario would bring the number to 6.2 million people lifted above the $2 per day poverty line and 2.5 million people lifted above the $1 per day level of extreme poverty.

It is useful to summarize what these models do and do not do (in addition to the assumptions discussed above):

- The models of "full" liberalization at the global level and negotiations rarely bring tariffs to zero or include all products;
- All gains are one-time changes in the level of GDP, not annual growth rates;
- This approach cannot provide estimates of the measures that now form the heart of global and regional trade agreements and the controversies surrounding them. There are no reliable ex-ante methods for analyzing the impact of the changes in intellectual property rules, foreign investment policy and so forth.

Shrinking policy space

The "final" deal in Hong Kong and later in Geneva in July of 2008 would have consisted of cuts in agricultural tariffs and subsidies in the developed world for cuts in manufacturing tariffs and services regulation by the developing world. The details of this bargain reflect that loss of policy space would indeed be significant, especially as taken as a whole with the UR.

Echoing some of what is found in the last chapter, Table 5.3 exhibits our illustrative toolbox of policies and examines the extent to which the catch up globalization policies in our toolbox would have been further constrained in the DDR.

Table 5.3. The shrinking of policy space in the DDR

Policy instrument	WTO
Goods trade	*
Tariff sequencing	
tax drawbacks	
Intellectual property	X
Limiting patent scope	X
Short patent timelines with exceptions	
Compulsory licenses	
Subsidies	X
Export	*
R&D	*
Distribution	*
Environment	
Cost of capital	
Foreign investment	X
Local content	X
Trade balancing	
Joint ventures	
Technology transfer	
R&D	
Employment of local personnel	
Tax concessions	
Pre-establishment "screening"	
Capital controls	
Other	*
Human capital	
Administrative guidance	
Movement of people	
Provision of infrastructure	

NAMA goods trade

In exchange for small benefits in terms of agricultural market access on the part of developed countries, developing countries were asked to open their manufacturing markets. From Hong Kong until Geneva the developing world, led by a coalition of developing countries with key manufacturing sectors who called themselves the "NAMA 11," saw the terms of rich country proposals for manufacturing market access as in violation of the development mandate and in violation of the principle of "less than full reciprocity." While agriculture proposals left numerous carve outs for rich countries and did not force them to cut into applied rates, under NAMA developing countries were asked to cut below their applied rates. The consequences would have been significant losses in tariff revenue, terms of trade losses and lost policy space.

Shrinking tariff revenue

The proposals in the Doha Round, from Hong Kong until talks collapsed in the summer of 2006, would have made some nations suffer major losses of government revenue and made it much more difficult to use tariffs for selectively fostering industry. For instance, in the nonagricultural market access (NAMA) negotiations developed countries proposed binding all tariff lines, lowering average tariffs by at least 30 percent, with such reductions on a tariff line by tariff line basis under a Swiss formula. Under a "likely" scenario this would lower the average developing country tariff from 12.5 percent to 5.9 percent for existing tariff lines, or from 12.5 percent to 9.2 percent if all lines became bound (de Córdoba, Laird and Vanzetti 2005).

Not only were the projections of the benefits in terms of market access small for the round, but the costs in terms of tariff revenue losses and policy space were very real.

These benefits would be met with significant costs. Using the same model as the World Bank, UNCTAD has published estimates of projected tariff revenue losses under the NAMA negotiations of the Doha Round for a Swiss formula scenario which resembles the likely Doha outcome – a coefficient of 10. These tariff revenue losses are shown with the World Bank benefit projections for the world and various regions and countries in Table 5.4.

While there is evidence that shifting from trade to consumption taxes can be better for welfare, in the real world such taxation schemes cost political capital, and in some cases may not even be possible. Indeed, it has been shown that tariffs may be preferable in developing countries with large informal sectors that cannot be taxed efficiently (Stiglitz and Emran 2004). Many developing countries rely on tariffs for more than one quarter of their tax revenue. For smaller nations with little diversification in their economies, tariff revenues

Table 5.4. Doha's hidden price tag

	(Billions of 2001 US dollars)			(Percent change) Terms of trade****
	WB "likely" scenario*	WB Doha scenario**	NAMA tariff losses***	
Developed	**79.9**	**31.7**	**38.0**	**−0.12**
Developing	**16.1**	**6.7**	**63.4**	**−0.74**
Selected developing regions				
Middle East and North Africa	−0.6	−0.1	7.0	−1.32
Sub-Saharan Africa	0.4	0.6	1.7	−0.83
Latin America and the Caribbean	7.9	2.4	10.7	−1.12
Selected countries				
Brazil	3.6	1.4	3.1	−0.18
India	2.2	2.2	7.9	−1.62
Mexico	−0.9	−0.7	0.4	−0.48
Bangladesh	−0.1	0.1	0.04	−0.58

    * Anderson and Martin (2005, table 12.14, scenario 7).
    ** Anderson and Martin (2005, table 12.14, scenario 7 with SSPs).
    *** de Córdoba and Vanzetti (2006, table 11).
**** Polaski (2006, table 3.4).

provide the core of government budgets. According to the South Centre, in the Dominican Republic, Guinea, Madagascar, Sierra Leone, Swaziland and Uganda tariff revenues are more than 40 percent of all government revenue in their countries (South Centre 2004).

Tariff revenue losses will be significant and even outweigh the benefits in some cases. Total tariff losses for developing countries under the NAMA could be $63.4 billion or almost four times the benefit. Africa, the Middle East and Bangladesh – areas with large informal economies and where tariff revenues are key for government revenues – are predicted to be net losers in terms of benefits, they will also suffer even larger losses in tariff revenues.

In this table only Brazil would reap benefits larger than the tariff revenue losses. However, while Brazil may gain $3.6 billion it will still lose $3.1 billion in tariff revenue. This will be the result of increased competition from imports into heavy industry. Such competition will be coupled with significant urban job losses in those industries. Although there may be modest job creation in

Brazil's soy country, few of those displaced workers will opt to move to the countryside. What's more, the Brazilian government will be hard pressed to tax the left over benefits that will flow to soy agribusiness to compensate industrial workers for their losses.

In a 2005 issue of *Foreign Affairs*, Jagdish Bhagwati (2005) commented that more attention needed to be paid to adjusting to tariff revenue losses in developing countries:

> If poor countries that are dependent on tariff revenues for social spending risk losing those revenues by cutting tariffs, international agencies such as the World Bank should stand ready to make up the difference until their tax systems can be fixed to raise revenues in other, more appropriate, ways. (12)

At present even the most ambitious "aid for trade" packages come nowhere near filling the gap in lost tariff revenue predicted by UNCTAD.

Declining terms of trade

A likely deal will also contribute to declining terms of trade for developing countries, the ratio of export to import prices. This measure is considered a crucial estimate of the extent to which a developing country is moving up the value chain in the global economy, away from primary production and into manufacturing or knowledge-based activities. Since the First World War many developing countries saw their terms of trade deteriorate. Declining terms of trade can accentuate balance-of-payments problems and make the need to diversify into other export products even more urgent.

Under a likely deal world prices for agricultural products increase and manufacturing prices decrease slightly or remain unchanged. According to the Carnegie Endowment for International Peace these price changes negatively affect the terms of trade for developing countries (see Table 5.4). The report explains that for many developing countries the rise in world prices for imported food and agricultural goods is countered with a decline in world prices for their light manufactured exports, such as apparel. This partly explains why Bangladesh, East Africa and the rest of Sub-Saharan Africa are projected to be worse off from the deal.

The tariff losses for NAMA would be four times the benefit. Of course, in formal economic terms it is looking at apples and oranges to compare revenue and welfare. For negotiators, who are representatives of governments, apples and oranges are both fruits. A government negotiator will be interested in whether they will be better off, and by what magnitude. They will also be interested in what losses in revenue will occur (if for no better reason than to understand that new revenue is needed through new tax policy). It should come as no surprise that nations that stood to gain very little (or actually lost) and stood to lose a great deal in tariff revenue would begin to get skeptical. Add that to the fact that domestic producers at home who would then have to compete with new imports would be pressuring them and negotiators would have to come up with many more benefits to make everyone better off.

A second area of concern under NAMA was the adoption in Hong Kong of a Swiss formula approach to industrial tariff cuts. Swiss formulae are scenarios that would allow higher tariffs to be cut more than lower tariffs. The formula is represented as follows:

$$t_1 = \frac{a * t_o}{a + t_o}$$

Where (t_o) is the initial tariff, (a) is the tariff "coefficient" that sets the highest possible tariff in the new schedule and (t_1) is the new tariff. Figure 5.1 illustrates how coefficients of 6 and 25 for developed and developing countries respectively (the coefficients plausible under a "likely scenario") would work.

In Figure 5.1 the horizontal axis is the initial tariff (t_o) and the vertical axis is the final or Doha tariff (t_1). Applying the Swiss formula with coefficients of 6 for developed countries and 25 for developing countries, the figure shows how higher tariffs are reduced more than lower tariffs. For developing countries,

Figure 5.1. Application of Swiss formula for NAMA negotiations

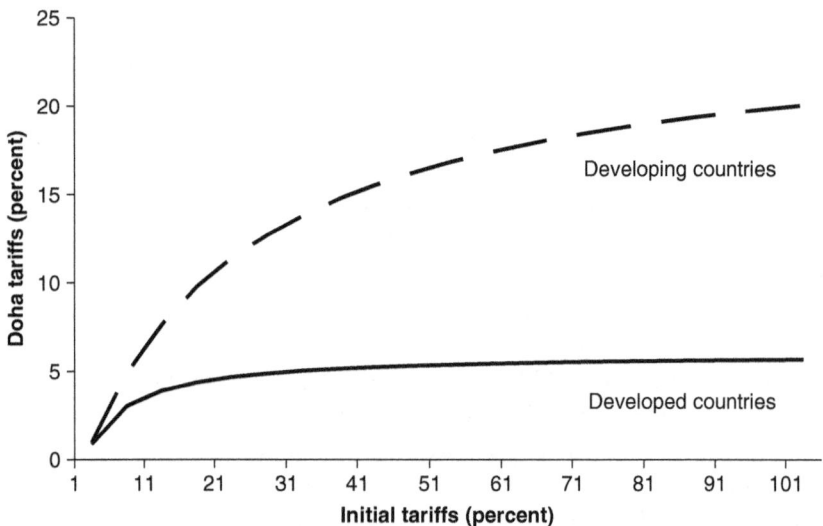

tariffs that were 101 percent are reduced to 20 percent $(25(101)/25+101)$, whereas for developed countries, where the coefficient would be 6, tariffs that were 101 percent would be reduced to just over 5 percent.

The fiscal costs of these tariff reductions will be significant. The coefficient under discussion during Hong Kong and the summer of 2006 was a coefficient of 22. The United Nations Conference on Trade and Development (UNCTAD) predicts that the losses in tariff revenue for developing countries would be approximately $63 billion. If all tariffs were eliminated under full liberalization, the losses would be $135.5 billion.

If such a scenario was accepted, the Swiss formula approach would have made tariff sequencing more difficult because higher tariffs would be cut deeper than lower tariffs. In a recent paper, Yilmaz Akyüz (2005) describes how many nations sequence tariffs for technological development.

Tariffs are introduced once a particular line of industry is entered and kept at their initial (maximum) levels for a certain period before being brought down at a constant rate as the industry matures. For the reasons already noted, technology-intensive industries have higher initial levels of protection and support than resource-based and labor-intensive manufacturing. As technological capacities are built successfully, subsequent shifts to more advanced sectors become relatively easier than the earlier move from labor-intensive to technology-intensive activities (Akyüz 2005, 26).

Binding at a line-by-line basis and reducing tariffs under a Swiss formula would make such sequencing much more difficult because nations would not be able to maintain relatively low average tariffs while having high tariffs in some lines and zero tariffs in others. Some developing nations, such as Brazil, India, Pakistan and others, have proposed NAMA reductions using a Swiss formula that sets a coefficient equivalent to the nation's average tariff. Brazil currently has an average tariff of 30 percent, India 19 percent and Pakistan 11 percent (de Córdoba, Laird and Vanzetti 2005). That would make numerous formulae possible and allow nations to be more varied – but very high tariffs would be difficult to maintain by the nature of the formula. Finally, the economic costs of lost tariff revenue, as shown earlier in the chapter, could be quite significant. There have not been proposals to change the safeguard mechanisms under the current round.

Services

The proposal regarding services that emerged in Hong Kong (and which was tabled in 2006) was that developing nations liberalize significantly more services sectors, especially financial services in places like Brazil and India. Developing nations were not necessarily opposed to this, indeed Brazil and India indicated as much in Hong Kong. However, developing countries argued for an emergency safeguard mechanism and for the liberalization of employment services in the North – both were rejected by developed countries.

Developing nations proposed that an emergency safeguard mechanism (ESM) be inserted into GATS, but developed nations have had a lukewarm response to such proposals. Instead, developed nations, led by the EU, proposed that developing nations quantify the number of service sectors they have and commit to liberalizing a minimum level of sectors – 50 percent of all sectors (developed countries would reduce 80 percent of their sectors). In the mode 3 negotiations (for foreign investment in services), the EU is pushing for 51 percent foreign equity holdings in domestic service sectors.

Developing countries did indeed have a proposal that would have yielded many more benefits for developed and developing countries alike. Developing countries proposed liberalizing employment services under the General Agreement in Trade and Services. This meant allowing for more visas for professional employees (such as software engineers from India) and temporary visas for low-skilled workers (such as apple pickers from Mexico). Studies have shown that the potential benefits of such liberalization could range between $150 billion and $300 billion on an annual basis, depending upon whether temporary work from developing countries amounted to 3 or 5 percent of industrial country workforces respectively (Winters et al. 2003). Another study that looked at the possibility of a 3 percent quota estimated that annual gains could be $200 billion annually (Rodrik 2011). The same study stresses the fact that such gains – which dwarf both the "likely" and full liberalization scenarios, go directly to those individuals in the developing world who need the funds the most because much of the gains are transferred through remittances.

Subsidies and Countervailing Measures (SCM)

Although not a major piece of the negotiations, some policy space was up for grabs under the SCM. As mentioned earlier the SCM allows for some subsidies that correct for market failures. These nonactionable subsidies are arguably more justified in economic terms because they can be used in second best settings to correct distortions in domestic and international markets (Hoekman and Kostecki 2000). The door to deploying such subsidies may be closing in the current negotiations.

Under Article 8 of the SCM, 3 types of subsidies were permitted "green light" subsidies – assistance for research and development, assistance to disadvantaged regions, assistance to promote the adaptation of existing facilities to new environmental regulations. Some nations were taking advantage of these provisions but the full potential of them was yet to be realized. However, ability to use such subsidies expired in the year 2000; the Doha Declaration provided the opportunity to negotiate the reinstatement and expansion of these subsidies but little progress was made (Aguayo and Gallagher 2009).

What Happened in Geneva, July 2008?

The Hong Kong Ministerial again ended without agreement. Since then there have been numerous "last ditch" efforts to conclude a deal. None of those efforts have led to a deal. Looming behind the talks as they drove on were two important factors: the loss of "fast track" negotiating authority in the United States, and elections in the US and beyond.

The United States Constitution puts the power of international economic relations such as the WTO in the hands of Congress. The US invented "fast track" (now referred to as "Trade Promotion Authority") as a vehicle to grant the president of the United States the ability to negotiate trade agreements on behalf of Congress for five-year increments. When a president negotiates a deal, Congress can pass it with a simple "yes" or "no" vote – rather than having the power to add on little amendments that might cause trading partners to want to renegotiate the deal. "Fast track" has now expired and it is not clear that a new US president will pass a new bill.

Thus Doha made a last attempt in 2008 to secure a deal. Most members went in good faith to try to get a deal. The thought was that a modest but fair deal was better than no deal at all. Toward the end game, the US and other developed nations would have cut applied agricultural tariffs from 15 percent on average to 11 percent. On agriculture, the US offered to cut its trade-distorting subsidies to $14.5 billion (well above current levels). Regarding manufacturing tariff reductions, developed country members agreed to apply an across-the-board Swiss formula coefficient (the lower the coefficient the deeper the cut) of 7 to 9 and developing countries agreed to three different ranges between 19 and 26 (the lower the coefficient the more exceptions each country can enjoy). Finally, many developing countries agreed in principle to liberalize their financial service sectors.

India and members of the G-33 proposed that if imports rise above 115 percent over a base period, developing nations should be allowed to impose Special Safeguard Measures (SSM) that are 25–30 percent over its bound duties on products taking zero cut. The Bush administration, however, refused to come down below a 140 percent trigger, a level India and other countries argued would make the mechanism virtually useless in most circumstances.

The NAMA 11,[9] a group of manufacturing centered developing countries headed by South Africa, was concerned over the movements in agriculture and in NAMA. According to interviews with NAMA 11 members, the "victory" of Hong Kong was to re-enshrine the concept of "less than full reciprocity" and that progress in the negotiations on NAMA and services would *follow* progress on agriculture. In the agriculture negotiations the developed countries agreed to cuts, but such cuts would not make countries cut below their applied rates of protection. What's more, developed countries were yet to table any specific consideration to cotton protections, an issue dear to Sub-Saharan African nations. Finally, the North rejected proposals for a SSM.

In the negotiations over NAMA, less than full reciprocity was being violated to an even higher degree. The Swiss formula and the coefficients proposed cuts would have made developing countries cut deeper than developed countries, and would have made developing countries cut into their applied rates of protection. Finally, the NAMA 11 was willing to accept such conditions as long as there be flexibilities whereby a nation could carve out certain sectors and protect them while largely adhering to the coefficients. Developed countries agreed to this only on condition of an "anti-concentration" clause that would have prohibited clustering flexibilities in a small number of sectors. NAMA 11 and other developing countries saw this as the whole point. They saw rich country demands as a policy of "do as we say, not as we do." They looked at the example of the US and European economies, and more recently, the economies of South Korea and China (all discussed in Chapter 3), all of which moved into the world marketplace slowly, protecting their major exporting industries with tariff shields in order to nurture them into world markets. China's computer maker, Lenovo, is a prime example. The company was created by the government and protected for years; it recently purchased IBM's PC division and is now a world leader in high technology electronics. Acer Computer from Taiwan and Hyundai and Kia Motors from South Korea followed similar paths.

The reason developing countries were less than enthusiastic to accept the deal that was on the table becomes clearer. The benefits would have been small (and negative for some countries), tariff losses would be high in terms of NAMA and developing countries were not able to obtain an ESM in services, nor liberalization in the movement of persons (the measure that would have brought the highest level of benefit), protections for their farmers and more.

Notes

1 "A Doha Scorecard: Will Rich Countries Once Again Leave Developing Countries as Beggars at the Feast?" Speech by Eveline Herfkens, Cancun 2003.
2 All projections of the benefits of the Doha Round in this chapter are found in Anderson and Martin (2005, tables 10, 12.14); Anderson et al. (2005). For a critical review of these estimates see Ackerman (2005).
3 The changes in estimates from 2003 to 2005 are due to modeling improvements and the fact that much trade liberalization has occurred since the last time estimates were

generated. Specifically, the World Bank updated their "base year" from 1997 to 2001. Such an exercise brings China's accession to the WTO into the base as a reform already achieved. The new versions of the models also incorporate the European Union's expansion, the expiration of the Multi-Fiber Agreement, and more detailed data on applied versus bound tariffs, including the effect of trade preferences and regional trade agreements.

4 New research by the Carnegie Endowment for International Peace using similar modeling exercises puts the potential gains to developing countries at $21.5 billion. See Sandra Polaski (2006, figures 3.1–3.8).

5 See Anderson et al. (2005).

6 See Hertel and Kenney (2006).

7 For estimates of services benefits, see Francois et al. (2003, table 4.4).

8 See note 3.

9 NAMA 11 – represents developing countries demanding a new mechanism to solve conflicts over non-tariff barriers to trade. The NAMA-11 members are Argentina, Bolivarian Republic of Venezuela, Brazil, Egypt, India, Indonesia, Namibia, Philippines, South Africa and Tunisia.

Chapter 6

TRADING AWAY THE LADDER? TRADE POLITICS AND ECONOMIC DEVELOPMENT IN THE AMERICAS

Over the past 20 years many nations from Latin America and the Caribbean (LAC) have signed and ratified free trade agreements with the United States. These agreements lock-in and expand the preferential access to the US market that LAC nations have enjoyed for some time. In exchange for preferential access to the largest economy in the world, LAC nations have agreed to provisions regarding financial services, intellectual property and foreign investment, and beyond that go far "deeper" than commitments under the World Trade Organization. This chapter builds on previous work (Gallagher 2008a; Gallagher and Thrasher 2010) and draws heavily from the deep insights of other scholars, especially Kenneth Shadlen of the London School of Economics (Shadlen 2006, 2008) to examine the extent to which those deeper commitments curtail the ability of LAC nations to deploy adequate policies to diversify their economies for development.

The first section of the chapter presents a theoretical framework regarding the political economy of signing US-style free trade agreements from a development perspective. Section two examines the extent to which recent treaties impact the ability of nations to deploy countercyclical and monetary policies. Section three discusses the extent to which these treaties grant sufficient policy space for industrial development. The final section summarizes the main arguments of the chapter and raises some political economy questions regarding why LAC nations are willing to forego so much more policy space than those same nations are willing to accept at the WTO.

Trade Politics and the Development Process

The politics of trade in nations that still hope to "catch up" with higher income nations needs to be treated differently than the political economy of trade in the developed world. In most mainstream discussions, the political

economy of trade is dominated by extensions of the Ricardian, Heckscher–
Ohlin and especially Stolper–Samuelson (S–S) models of trade, to the
political realm. Such extensions are inadequate for analyzing countries in the
development process because developing countries need to *change* the structure
of their economies toward sectors where they do not yet enjoy a comparative
advantage. Traditional economic and political analysis examines or assumes
a situation whereby a nation seeks to improve prospects for sectors where it
already has a comparative advantage. Any theoretical approach that starts
from a static perspective then will be very limited.

Textbook neoclassical trade theory stresses the need to liberalize those
sectors where a nation enjoys a comparative advantage in the present.
Under a trade treaty, exports will expand in those sectors where a nation
enjoys a comparative advantage. Extensions of S–S models refer to those
sectors as the "winners." The "losers" are those domestic sectors that have to
face import competition with trading partners that have a static comparative
advantage in a given good at the time. The "winners" are obviously strong
advocates for the treaty and the losers are more often than not, against.
Most mainstream political analysis thus analyzes how the winners politically
organize in order to get a treaty passed – at both the international and
domestic level. When the theory is taken at face value and the treaty does
not pass, these analysts assume a collective action problem exists whereby
the losses to the losers are seen to be highly concentrated but the gains to
the winners are too dissipated (see Aggarwal et al. 2004). In addition to the
producer surplus that could be gained through exporting new goods where
the nation has a comparative advantage, consumers experience a welfare
effect from cheaper imports. Yet a collective action problem exists because
the consumer beneficiaries are too scattered to organize in their interest,
and thus a coalition among the consumer and producer beneficiaries is not
strong enough to defeat the protectionists that do not want to face import
competition.

All this economic and political activity takes place in an assumed world
where comparative advantages are static and that nations literally "enjoy" the
comparative advantages they hold at the time of a trade negotiation. The
process of economic development is to fundamentally change the structure
of an economy from one based largely on a handful of primary products
to a more diversified economy that can be competitive in a variety of
commodities as well as in industry and the newly dynamic services sector.
That means that a nation wishes to develop new comparative advantages in
the future. There is a long history of theoretical perspectives on diversification
or building dynamic comparative advantage that is much too vast to cover
here (see Lall 2005). What is common throughout this literature is the need for

the state to play a role in economic diversification because the market will not automatically bring about such diversification.

Thus, there are at least three key issues that need to be overcome in such a context. First, nations have to make a "choice" between static and dynamic development when considering trade negotiations. Second, domestic politics in the developing country will tend to favor the choice of a trade treaty because the winners of a dynamic approach are by definition politically active and powerful in the future, not the present when the negotiations will take place. Third, if a treaty is signed it may constrain the ability of a developing nation to deploy policies for dynamism.

During trade negotiations between a (highly) developed nation such as the US and LAC nations still seeking to industrialize, the US seeks to solidify its current comparative advantages in high-tech manufacturing, services and (artificially so) in agriculture by securing more market access in LAC for those goods and "protecting" that access through further regulations (in the treaty) on intellectual property, investment rules, services regulation and more. Those sectors in the US are highly organized politically and can overcome collective action problems by spending enormous amounts of time and resources on campaigns to convince citizens of the benefits of a treaty tilted in the favor of US interests (Mayer 1998).[1]

When a less-developed country hoping to build dynamic comparative advantage enters a negotiation with a higher income nation like the US, one would think there is cause for concern. A trade treaty that grants market access to the US for the sectors listed above would render the corresponding sectors "losers" that could never compete with their US counterparts. Combining the collective action idea with the dynamics of development then, one needs to think of collective action issues over time. The short-term winners (owners of primary commodities or light manufacturing) are highly concentrated and lobby strenuously for a government to pursue an agreement with the US and to ratify it at home when signed. But the longer run winners (those sectors that will be dynamic in the future and future consumers) are by their very nature weak, dissipated, or even nonexistent in the short term in the sense of their ability to participate in current politics and are thus the "losers" of a trade treaty.

A short illustrative example may be helpful. If the United States and South Korea entered into negotiations in 1970, South Korea would probably have a comparative advantage in rice and the United States would probably have had a comparative advantage in cars. From a static perspective one would expect South Korean rice producers pushing for the deal, as well as US carmakers. South Korean automakers and US rice growers were probably less keen on the idea. Simple calculations, however, could show in a static sense that the gains to the rice growers would outweigh the losses to the South Korean auto sector. Fast forward 30 years later and in actual negotiations between these two countries South Korea wants to protect its rice sector and the US wants to protect its car sector. In South Korea's case they deployed a blend of industrial policies to develop a world class auto sector (Amsden 2001). In 1970 that sector, though formidably strong in 2010, did not exist or was too fledgling to be politically active. If South Korea had signed an agreement in 1970 they might not have an auto sector now. Implicitly, South Korea decided that it would incur sometimes heavy costs of waiting to climb the technology ladder. South Korea had to put together the capabilities to develop an auto sector, beating the odds to have a comparative advantage. For those 35 years they had to forego some growth that would have occurred when they were trying to develop the auto sector. They could have both exported more rice and imported better cars during that whole period. South Korea chose not to do that, overcoming the collective action problem that the political forces supporting long-run productive capacities were not as strong. South Korea's 2010 growth dynamics are greatly benefited from having industrial shipping, auto and other high value-added sectors.

Trade treaties with nations still needing to develop comparative advantages add yet another obstacle for nations hoping to diversify for development. In the last section of the chapter I examine how the problems of assuming static comparative advantage and collective action problems interact with other political forces to (partly) explain why LAC continue to sign treaties with the US that may not be in the interest of long-run growth in LAC.

Macro Impacts of FTAs in the Americas: Stability and Growth

Over the past two decades there has been a sixfold increase in the number of FTAs in the world economy. Nowhere has this proliferation been more prevalent than in Latin America (LAC), where 33 of the 39 countries belong to at least one FTA (World Bank 2005).

Spearheading a great deal of the recent wave of FTAs in the region have been agreements with the United States. At this writing, the US has completed agreements (though not always ratified) with Chile, Colombia, Costa Rica, Dominican Republic, El Salvador, Guatemala, Honduras, Mexico, Nicaragua, Panama and Peru. Discussions for a Free Trade Area of the Americas (FTAA) commenced in 1993 and included all LAC nations except for Cuba. These discussions have been put on hold and perhaps even put away forever.

This section of the chapter shows that by all accounts the economic gains from FTAs in LAC are smaller than if LAC pursued global trade liberalization under the WTO. Moreover, it shows that the agreements will bring small gains in terms of growth, worsen current account positions, deplete tariff revenue, appreciate the exchange rate and worsen the terms of trade for LAC nations. Finally, it will be shown that measures such as prudential capital controls that can be used to buffer some of these negative effects are not permitted under US trade deals.

As noted throughout this book, most estimates of the gains from trade come from the computable equilibrium (CGE) models. The most recent and well-known CGE estimates of the gains from FTAs have been calculated by the World Bank and published in *Global Economic Prospects* (2005). In that report the bank's CGE projections use a 2001 base year and perform an experiment where they simulate changes in economies in 2001 without trade policy changes and then with trade policy proposals at the global and regional levels.

Under full global trade liberalization the World Bank estimates that the gains from trade would be $263.2 billion, or a one-time increase in global GDP of 0.8 percent in 2015. More than half of those gains go to developed countries, and LAC would receive $24.6 billion. It should be noted that the gains from global trade liberalization are relatively small at this point for developing nations, but even smaller under FTAs. Under both the FTA scenarios developing countries stand to lose, $21.5 billion and $6.6 billion respectively. If LAC signed FTAs with all of the large developed and developing countries the gains would be merely $9 million. If they signed FTAs with developed countries without the large developing countries participating the LAC gains would be $3.4 billion. In other words, the benefits of FTAs for LAC countries would range from four tenths of one cent per day in 2015, to one and three-quarters cents per day in 2015. That is for the countries that gain. However, as can be seen by the single country estimates that are available, Mexico and Brazil could be losers under these scenarios.

Table 6.1 presents recent estimates regarding US treaties with various LAC nations. In these cases we can see that the welfare gains are very small (and sometimes negative).

The third column of the table exhibits that tariff losses are estimated to be $1.3 billion for these nations. Tariffs as percent of tax revenue are on average 10 percent for LAC. These losses cited above represent a loss of 10–23 percent of tariff revenue. This is no small amount in the wake of the financial crisis where funds are needed to put in place countercyclical macroeconomic policy.

In a study for the Inter-American Development Bank, Giordano et al. (2010) state that these treaties are expected to worsen current account balances and exchange rate positions. According to these authors, GDP is expected to increase by one half of one percent due to the treaty, while imports increase

Table 6.1. Welfare benefits vs. tariff losses

	Welfare gain*	Tariff losses**
	(Millions of 2004 dollars)	
Country		
Colombia	−163	633
Peru	−43	195
Costa Rica	201	115
El Salvador	171	82
Guatemala	296	178
Honduras	80	80
Nicaragua	48	21
Total	**590**	**1,304**

* For CAFTA countries: Hilaire and Yang (2004, 19).
* For Colombia and Peru: Durán Lima, de Miguel and Schuschny (2007, 88).
** For tariff losses: Tanzi, Barreix and Villela (2008, 34).

more than exports (thus accounting for most of the gains as consumer surplus gains), the exchange rate appreciates and terms of trade worsen.

All US treaties also prohibit the use of capital controls as prudential measures to cool exchange rate appreciation and to remedy balance-of-payments problems. The free transfer of funds to and from the US is a core principle of US BITs and FTAs, as well as those of most other capital-exporting countries. Argentina violated such principles after its 2001–2002 crisis and was subject to numerous claims.

Of all the treaties the US has signed there is only one clear exception to this rule, the balance-of-payments exception found in NAFTA. Article 2014(1) can be invoked when the host state experiences "serious balance of payments difficulties, or the threat thereof." Like similar exceptions at the WTO and OECD, use of the exception must be temporary, nondiscriminatory and be consistent to the IMF Articles of Agreement (thus capital controls can only be aimed at capital account transactions unless approved by the IMF).

Chile is a nation that has deployed capital controls to some success. The US negotiated FTAs with Chile and Singapore (who had also used capital controls in the wake of the 1997 Asian crisis) at the turn of the century, both came into force in 2004. The limits in the US model on capital controls became major sticking points for both Chile and Singapore. In fact, during the negotiations with Chile, USTR head Robert Zoellick had to intervene with the finance minister of Chile to salvage the negotiations over this issue. During those negotiations the US negotiated a "compromise" that, with some variation, has been used in agreements with Singapore, Peru and Colombia. Interestingly, however, it has not become a matter of practice. Such a cooling off period was not included in the 2004 Model BIT nor the FTAs with DR–CAFTA, Panama and others.

As noted in the second chapter, these "cooling off" provisions are rife with controversy and give a nation limited room if any to maneuver.

It should also be noted that these provisions are not mutual. The cooling off period is only for investors suing "a Party other than the United States." Finally, the annexes agree that once the claim is brought, only "actual reduction of the value of the transfer" counts as a loss (United States of America 2004). Loss of profits, loss of business and other similar consequential or incidental damages cannot be recovered. All of these agreements include some exceptions to the annex, instances where the cooling off period and limitation on damages does not apply: payments on current transactions, on transfers associated with equity investments and loan or bond payments.

The Microeconomic Costs of FTAs with the US: Endogenous Productive Capacity

Economic theory states that when the market fails, policy instruments should be deployed to correct the distortions created by private markets (Lipsey and Lancaster 1956). This theory is referred to as the "second best" theory, and states that government policy can offset market failures. Some economists have rightly pointed out that the lifting of a tariff is not the equivalent of eliminating distortions. Indeed, lifting tariffs can at time accentuate distortions (Kowalczyk 1989, 2002). In such an environment, some development economists call for government intervention used in a careful manner are one of a myriad tools that can work as second best solution to the distortions occurring through trade liberalization. Indeed, in an environment rife with market failure it has been argued that it is the role of government to precisely "get the prices wrong" in the short and intermediate term to combat the fact that late industrializing countries would not be able to advance given present market structures. In other words, market failures send the wrong signals to firms in developing countries and have to be combated with market failures themselves in order to set a new equilibrium (Amsden 1992a; Chang 2002; Rodrik 2005).

Table 6.3 exhibits the core policies used by developed and developing countries to correct for market failures and jumpstart development. It should be noted that LAC's record with these types of policies was weaker relative to other nations that used them. Per capita growth rates when experimenting with such policy in the 1970s, for instance, were 3.3 percent annually in LAC compared to 5.2 percent in East Asia. Relative to their performance under the neoliberal period however, no country except Chile has had a faster growth rate since 1980 then during the period 1950 to 1980.

Table 6.3 shows the extent to which the core industrial policies used to correct market failures are permissible under the WTO and FTAs between the United States and LAC. An "X" marks a situation that is not permitted under trade rules, an asterisk "*" indicates that such an instrument has been proposed to be outlawed under the ongoing Doha negotiations but is not yet prohibited, and a blank space indicates cases where the "policy space" remains to use such an instrument.

The table reveals that there is still considerable policy space under the WTO for industrial development, a finding that is well documented (see Shadlen 2005a). However, in almost every case LAC nations are "trading away" their ability to deploy such policies in FTAs with the United States. As will be discussed in the next section, this is particularly puzzling given that the gains are relatively small of such FTAs and given that LAC nations have coalesced to oppose proposals to eliminate similar measures under the WTO.

Successful industrial policy relied on tariff protection and subsidies to help foster national firm capabilities (Amsden 2001). Under FTAs between the US and LAC nations, most tariff lines are negotiated to zero over a period of time. This constrains the ability of nations to perform tariff sequencing where they chose not to bind certain sectors or bind them at a high level. This left room to apply tariffs at a higher level for certain sectors during periods of industry support and reducing or shifting them to other sectors later in time (Akyüz 2005). There is still considerable room for such policy under the WTO; however, the formula being negotiated for manufacturing tariffs under the Doha Round will make it considerably more difficult (Gallagher 2008b).

As for subsidization, Table 6.2 shows the constrain that FTAs place on the ability of LAC nations to subsidize domestic sectors relative to the WTO. There is a burgeoning discussion regarding the "comeback" of industrial policy in LAC (Peres 2006). The new industrial policy has been referred to as "open economy" industrial policy because it relies on providing credit to domestic firms to combat the market failures regarding the cost of capital (Melo 2001; Schrank and Kurtz 2005). According to Melo these instruments include loans for working capital, discrete capital goods, project finance, export credit, overseas marketing and export finance – some of which are discriminatory as they favor domestic firms. Schrank and Kurtz perform a

Table 6.2. Deepening commitments under PTAs

Policy instrument	WTO	LAC PTAs
Goods trade		
Tariff sequencing	*	X
Tax drawbacks		
Intellectual property		
Limiting patent scope	X	X
Short patent timelines with exceptions	X	X
Compulsory licenses		X
Subsidies		
Export	X	X
R&D	*	X
Distribution	*	X
Environment	*	X
Cost of capital		
Foreign investment		
Local content	X	X
Trade balancing	X	X
Joint ventures		X
Technology transfer		X
R&D		X
Employment of local personnel		X
Tax concessions		
Pre-establishment "screening"		X
Capital controls		X
Other		
Human capital		
Administrative guidance		
Movement of people	*	X
Provision of infrastructure		

regression analysis and find that those LAC countries that deploy a larger share of this family of industrial policies perform better in terms of exports. The WTO has recently begun to crack down on export credits (see the recent Brazil–US cotton case) and many of the FTAs in the region have a financial services sector that explicitly mentions export credits and loans as actionable.

Loose intellectual property rights were core strategies used by developed and developing countries alike in order to gain access to new technologies and practices. Late-comer developers limited the areas of activity where patents (referred to as patent scope) were granted to increase technological diffusion and development to national firms. What's more, late-comers allowed for shorter patent periods (for foreign firms) so ideas were diffused into the public realm more quickly. Table 6.2 is misleading here because it implies that there is little difference between the WTO and FTAs in LAC. Indeed, Shadlen (2005a) argues that "developing countries that enter into regional-bilateral agreements with the US typically accept obligations in the area of IPRs that go far beyond what is required as WTO members" (767). Under FTAs the ability to limit patent scope is indeed restricted under both scenarios as depicted in Table 6.4, but under FTAs the ability to limit patent scope is less flexible. What's more, while the WTO grants patent protection to an invention for 20 years, FTAs in the region typically include clauses requiring extensions beyond 20 years. Regarding compulsory licenses nations would use these instruments to lower prices, encourage foreign firms to source locally and gain access to knowledge. Under the WTO countries can largely determine the grounds for compulsory licensing. Under FTAs, compulsory licenses are limited to national emergencies. These fairly drastic differences led Shadlen (2005b) to conclude that:

> On all three of the dimensions used to IP management – government's abilities to determine which knowledge becomes private property, to provide for exceptions to patent-holder's exclusive rights, and to hasten arrival of the time that private knowledge enters the public domain – FTAs place significantly more burdensome and onerous obligations on developing countries than TRIPS does. (27)

In addition to the policy space for industrial development, intellectual property rules in FTAs make it more difficult to address public health in a nation. For instance, whereas under the WTO states have obligations regarding the treatment of test data (giving local generic pharmaceutical firms access to trial data allows them to produce generics in a more timely and less costly fashion) the US requires a minimum of five years of data exclusivity in FTAs (Shadlen 2005a). A recent study on the impacts of US intellectual property rules on an FTA found that medicine prices in Jordan increased 20 percent after the signing of the US–Jordan FTA. In addition, the study found that data exclusivity has stalled the development of generic drug competitors for 79 percent of the drugs newly introduced by 21 foreign pharmaceutical firms between 2002 and mid-2006, that otherwise would have been available in an inexpensive, generic form. The study also found that:

> Additional expenditures for medicines with no generic competitor, as a result of enforcement of data exclusivity by multinational drug companies, were between $6.3m and $22.04m. These expenditures have required that both public health system and individuals pay higher prices for many new medicines that are needed to treat serious non-communicable diseases (NCDs), such as hypertension, asthma, diabetes, and mental illness. For example, new medicines to treat diabetes and heart disease cost anywhere from two to six times more in Jordan than in Egypt, where there are no TRIPS-plus barriers. (Oxfam 2007, 2)

A study of quinolones in India found that the annual welfare losses to the Indian economy were $450 million. Eleven percent of those losses accrued to domestic producers and the rest to Indian consumers. In contrast, the profit gains to foreign producers were only $53 million per year (Chaudhuri et al. 2004).

Foreign direct investment (FDI) has been equally important in obtaining access to knowledge and technology. Many nations require joint ventures between foreign and local firms and/or perform research and development so that local firms gain access to know-how and production processes. Others require that a certain proportion of nationals be employed in the firm or that certain amounts of inputs by the foreign firms be purchased from local firms. Perhaps most important is the fact that nations under the WTO can "screen" foreign firms before they move to their country. This is referred to "pre-establishment rights." Post-establishment a nation has to treat a foreign firm as equally as it does a national firm (national treatment), but pre-establishment a nation has leeway to negotiate with foreign firms over the development of technological capabilities. It is interesting to note that nations in LAC, when negotiating FTAs amongst themselves, tend to grant each other the flexibility of screening, but under FTAs between LAC and the United States the US insists that national treatment is extended to the pre-establishment phase of foreign investing as well (Haslam 2004). The WTO has deemed requiring local content standards illegal, but virtually all of these other instruments are still permissible. Ironically, under FTAs developed countries often use rules of origin clauses to implicitly require for US "local content" purchases but this is seldom permitted by developing countries. China (the largest recipient of FDI in the world in 2005) is notorious for using many of these instruments that are permissible under the WTO to build local technological capabilities. FTAs constrain the ability of nations to use all of the instruments in Table 6.2

except for the ability to grant tax concessions to foreign firms. What's more, most (if not all) FTAs restrict the ability of nations to impose capital controls on foreign portfolio investment.

Another aspect of investment components of FTAs with the US is that they deploy an "investor-state" dispute system rather than a state-to-state system like that of the WTO. Whereas in the WTO a firm that had been damaged by a particular policy has to petition its national government to file a claim against the nation that has imposed damages, under US FTAs (like US BITs) the firm can directly sue the host nation for damage. Mexico has faced $1.7 billion in such claims since the signing of NAFTA (CPA 2007).

Last but not least, nations have relied on a relatively flexible global labor regime at different periods of time. Many of the East Asian nations sent their best and brightest to Western universities and firms to learn and work. These individuals would then return home to contribute to government labs or national firms (Kim and Nelson 2000). The easing of labor mobility rules is one of the foremost demands of developing countries at both the WTO and FTAs. Indeed, according to official estimates by the World Bank the benefits of a relatively small opening for labor in the developed world would bring over three times the benefits (more than $300 billion) to the developing world (Winters et al. 2003).

According to Table 6.3, LAC nations signing agreements with the United States can solely deploy tax drawbacks, human capital and infrastructure investments and administrative support to local firms to build productive capacity. Such measures are not seen as sufficient to foster industrial development in the twenty-first century (Rodrik 2005).

The Political Economy of Trade Agreements in the Americas

The previous sections have shown that the gains from FTAs in the Americas are relatively small and that the costs could be considerably high. If this is true, then why is LAC one of the most proliferate regions in terms of FTAs? Economic theory and the popular press would lead one to believe that LAC negotiators are acting rationally when signing the slate of trade agreements discussed in this chapter. This section of the chapter demonstrates that the collective action issues discussed earlier – as well as "power" and ideas – may go a longer way to explaining the political economy of trade agreements in the Americas than more traditional approaches.

Of course there are political forces at work that partly explain why LAC signs so many trade deals. The static winners in both the US and in LAC of trade agreements are very concentrated and politically strong in the present. They create alliances at home and abroad to push for such treaties. But there is more to it than that. In addition to these static interest-based explanations, LAC nations sign agreements because they are in a rat race whereby they feel the need to keep access to the US before a neighbor does (the "hub and spoke" effect), because of asymmetric bargaining power in the negotiations, because of ideological reasons and because of the collective action problem identified earlier.

Economic theory, and political economy in a liberal context, views trade treaties as providing public goods that bring benefits to each actor involved in the negotiation. Therefore, the creation of such regimes is a result of the actors involved working rationally, while acknowledging that the distribution of benefits could be unequal (Gilpin 1987). This notion can only partially explain why LAC has been signing FTAs with the US. Yes, of course it is in the interest of each nation to maintain access to the largest economy in the world, but the terms of such access seem to have little flexibility built into them.

Hubs and spokes: The rat race for access to the US market

A variant of neoclassical trade theory provides useful insight about the gains from patchwork FTAs such as those that are occurring in the hemisphere. While acknowledging that the gains from global trade are larger, Kowalczyk and Wonnacott (1992) have demonstrated that in a world of negotiating numerous FTAs – rather than global negotiations or even a larger Free Trade Area of the Americas – nations will see it as in their interest to sign an agreement before their geographical neighbors, so as to capture benefits from their rivals. The authors show formally that a nation's income can increase if it signs an FTA with a large economy such as the US (which they call a "hub") and potentially decrease if others sign with the large economy and the particular nation does not. If a nation negotiates an FTA with a large "hub" economy (and others do not) they can experience both a volume of trade increase and see their terms of trade improve. Reductions in tariffs on both sides of the negotiation increases the volume of trade between the two nations. Terms of trade may increase as well because the participating nation (which they call a "spoke") will experience higher prices for its exports.

For those nations that do not participate the opposite can be true – they can experience a reduction in trade volumes due to not participating in the agreement and a terms of trade deterioration because the their import and export prices might be higher relative to participating nations. The hub and spoke theory is difficult to model and generate empirical results from, but the framework does indicate when such a race will benefit or cost a nation engaging. However, if one looked at early CGE estimates of Mexico's entry into NAFTA, most put the gains at approximately three percent of GDP (see Stanford 2003). This theory can help explain why many nations not only see it as in their rational interest to enter into a FTA with the US, but to do it early. However, one cannot be sure that the gains will be positive.

FTAs are mini "grand bargains" where the US exchanges market access for many of the measures that may be "costly" if removed from domestic policy toolkit. However, the benefits of market access are perceived as outweighing the costs of losing policy space and trade diversion. This is especially true given that the counterfactual of losing access to the US market could be quite damaging for many countries and that there is a possibility that it can be costly to lose out to neighboring nations on getting into the US market first.

Older trading arrangements with LAC were under the Generalized System of Preferences and were unilateral in nature. In other words, the US granted preferential access to the nation and demanded little in return. Under contemporary FTAs the negotiations are premised on "reciprocity" where measures are exchanged. Given that few individual LAC nations offer much market access to the US, negotiations (from the perspective of US interests) can be seen as maintaining access to the US market in exchange for the reform of domestic regulatory standards in the developing country in such a manner that will favor (or at least level the playing field for) US firms (Shadlen 2006). What's more, hub and spoke theories and the counterfactual of potentially losing a nation's preference suggest that it may be even more in the interest of a nation to enter into an agreement with the US.

Market power, political power

As is abundantly clear from the previous discussions, the size and dynamism of the US market plays very strongly in forming the "rational" decisions of LACs when it comes to FTAs. Economic realists differ from liberals in stressing that it is the very power of the US market and its negotiating body that constrains the set of "rational" policies that countries like LACs can choose from. What's more, especially in the case of FTAs between the US and LAC, there is a question regarding whether both sides have positive gains. This section of the chapter takes a closer look at the nature of the asymmetry in bargaining power between the US and its trade partners in LAC and discusses the negotiations through such a lens.

Albert O. Hirschman's 1945 classic *National Power and the Structure of Foreign Trade* argued that a nation can exert its power over weaker nations through foreign trade. In a negotiation between a large economy and a smaller one the nation with the larger economy has the upper hand. Thus, the negotiation becomes one over the extent of the conditions that the larger economy will put on the smaller economy in return for access to the larger economy. With this framework in mind, consider the relative differences between the US and LAC nations in terms of market size: on average the US economy is over six thousand times as large as its trading partners and US income is on average over sixteen times those in LAC.

It has been convincingly argued that such power asymmetries are accentuated in the case of LAC because the US has dangled the loss of a nation's GSPs as a consequence of not entering into an FTA (Zoellick 2005). Many of the GSP systems have been in place for over twenty years and have determined the export profile of many nations. Building on earlier work by Gruber (2001) and Moe (2005) that argues that weaker nations participate in institutions that may not be in their interests, Shadlen (2007) argues that many LAC countries negotiate FTAs with the US where they trade away significant development measures out of a concern that they would be shut out of the US market. Thus, Shadlen contends that US economic power provides a choice set that is not a choice between an FTA or no FTA, but a choice between an FTA or no FTA when a neighbor receives an FTA and the nation in question potentially loses its preferential access to the US market. The US can assert a power constrained choice set, as Shadlen argues, because of the asymmetry of bargaining and market power.

These power asymmetries put hub and spoke arguments in a different light. Yes it may be rational for a nation to partake in an FTA under such conditions, but the power of the US has constrained the choice set of the nations negotiating with the US. Nicola Phillips (2005) writes:

The ideological dimensions of the regional project are often overlooked in a focus on the technical details of trade negotiations and the political bargaining processes under way in the region, but they are crucial to an understanding of the nature and the politics of the emerging regional economic regime. More specifically, [...] the US-led approach of a distinctly "hub and spoke" set of regionalist arrangements, as a key means by which to capture control of the governance agenda and to ensure that the regional economic regime takes a form consistent US interests and preferences. The growing prioritization to bilateralism has become the predominant strategy to this end. The leverage afforded to the US by the bilateral negotiation of trade agreements acts to stimulate primary influence over the shape of the rules that constitute the regime, and the primary functions associated with the task of its governance, firmly in the agencies of the US State. (3)

To illustrate this point Shadlen calculates an index of "Political Trade Dependence," to demonstrate that the LAC countries for whom exports receiving preferential access under GSP constitute the largest share of total exports are the most likely to sign FTAs with the US. The measure of political trade dependence is reproduced for each country and is the share of a country's total exports that enter the US under preferential schemes. Countries with high scores on the scale appear most eager to establish FTAs with the US. For example, all of the Andean countries negotiating FTAs and the six countries that signed DR–CAFTA are all above the median (Honduras, the DR and Nicaragua are all 300 percent or more above the mean). The next column calculates trade dependence (percentage of a nation's exports to the US over total exports) and shows that many of the same nations are very dependent on the US for all their exports.

In terms of the domestic politics that form the preferences of states, column 3 of Table 6.3 exhibits the percentage of total exports that go to the US for each LAC nation where data is available. On average over one third of all LAC exports go to the US and for countries like Mexico it is well over 75 percent. Behind these exports are very significant domestic coalitions pushing for opportunities to expand such exports – and certainly not lose such access (Thacker 2000). Juxtaposed with such short-term incentives the kinds of firms and general welfare improvements that might result from many of the policies "traded away" for market access are at a disadvantage in domestic politics.

Numerous studies have examined the role of power, interests and ideas in Latin American trade politics with respect to the United States. However, the majority of these analyses focus on just one of these factors and seldom acknowledge the relative importance of other independent variables. This last section of the chapter synthesizes the disparate literature on the political economy factors that determine why LAC nations sign agreements with the United States under the terms they do. In a more formal sense, if signing an agreement is a dependent variable, what are the independent variables that determine a signature and how might we think about the relative importance of each factor?

An interesting counterfactual is to look at how many LAC behave when in larger coalitions and among themselves. Paradoxically, many LAC nations have fought hard to preserve the right to deploy core industrial strategies in WTO coalitions while at the same time "trade them away" in FTAs with the United States. In the earlier days of the WTO's Doha Round, developed nations proposed numerous measures that would reduce the policy space for deploying loose intellectual property rules, enforcing policies for foreign investment that would create linkages to the domestic economy and so forth. Argentina, Bolivia, Brazil, Chile, Colombia, Costa Rica, Cuba, Ecuador,

Table 6.3. Asymmetric bargaining power between the US and LAC?

Country	Political trade dependence	Exports to US	GDPUS/ GDP	(GDP/cap) US/(GDP/ cap)	GDPUS/ GDP	Income US/ income
Bahamas*	-	77.5%	200633%	215%	2,006	2
Nicaragua	31.4%	29.3%	242764%	4305%	2,428	43
Dominican Republic	26.7%	40.2%	48032%	1412%	480	14
Honduras	21.2%	36.4%	161081%	3716%	1,611	37
St Kitts and Nevis	18.1%	71.2%	2908546%	470%	29,085	5
Haiti	12.4%	86.4%	267035%	7537%	2,670	75
Costa Rica	11.9%	49.7%	61042%	859%	610	9
Guatemala	10.8%	26.7%	49841%	1997%	498	20
Bolivia	9.3%	13.9%	115216%	3428%	1,152	34
Peru	8.7%	24.8%	18500%	1709%	185	17
Belize	8.5%	50.6%	1127668%	1017%	11,277	10
Trinidad and Tobago	8.3%	42.3%	115794%	523%	1,158	5
Uruguay	8.3%	8.6%	49267%	581%	493	6
Ecuador	7.9%	38.3%	58591%	2564%	586	26
El Salvador	7.7%	18.7%	73652%	1653%	737	17
Colombia	4.9%	43.4%	11574%	1737%	116	17
Grenada	4.3%	38.5%	2507688%	902%	25,077	9
Brazil	3.8%	24.7%	1614%	998%	16	10
Guyana	3.7%	33.2%	1350836%	3531%	13,508	35
Jamaica	3.6%	33.0%	120732%	1102%	1,207	11
Venezuela	2.3%	56.4%	8123%	705%	81	7
St Vincent and the Grenadines	2.2%	2.6%	2938301%	1200%	29,383	12
St Lucia	2.1%	17.6%	1504828%	833%	15,048	8
Dominica	2.0%	6.1%	3787380%	944%	37,874	9
Barbados	1.9%	14.9%	-	-	-	-
Panama	1.9%	47.5%	84185%	887%	842	9
Chile	1.8%	18.6%	12560%	687%	126	7

(Continued)

Table 6.3. Continued

Country	Political trade dependence	Exports to US	GDPUS/ GDP	(GDP/cap) US/(GDP/ cap)	GDPUS/ GDP	Income US/ income
Argentina	1.0%	10.9%	3622%	473%	36	5
Paraguay	0.8%	3.0%	124114%	2438%	1,241	24
Suriname	0.5%	21.0%	1055490%	1618%	10,555	16
Antigua and Barbuda	0.1%	19.0%	1428627%	388%	14,286	4
Mexico	0.1%	88.7%	1695%	588%	17	6

El Salvador, Guatemala, Mexico, Paraguay, Peru and Venezuela all opposed the further constraining of policy space at the Cancun Ministerial of the Doha Round. Yet of these countries, Chile, Colombia, Costa Rica, El Salvador, Guatemala, Mexico and Peru have all signed FTAs with the United States which ban the very measures they fought hard to protect under the WTO (Narlikar and Tussie 2004). What's more, Phillips (2005) shows that many LAC nations objected to much of the initial FTAA agenda "virtually without exception, LAC negotiators initially adhered to the principal that an FTAA process should be merely 'WTO-compatible'" (9). Finally, Haslam (2004) shows that when nations from LAC sign bilateral investment treaties with each other they allow for a great deal more flexibility in terms of policy space than what they end up signing in deals with the US.

The "power" of ideas

Previous analyses attempting to explain why LAC nations engage in so many FTAs with the US have somewhat discounted the fact that neoliberal ideas and ideology have permeated LAC over the past 25 years more, perhaps, than in any other developing region. Goldstein and Keohane (1993) have argued that if actors do not know the outcome of a particular policy decision they will resort to beliefs that will help them estimate the causal effects of their actions. By the time the majority of FTAs were under negotiations, neoliberal presidents were in power and were backed by fully (or near fully) transformed bureaucracies. Such elites were not in favor of the policies that were being "traded away" in the first place. Indeed for them negotiating FTAs was win–win. They received permanent or improved market access with the US and were able to use the FTA to push through reforms that they wanted to enact (but perhaps couldn't yet domestically) anyway.

There have been numerous studies in the sociology literature documenting the spread of neoliberal ideas throughout the Americas. Indeed, there is a considerable literature on how the "technopols" played a significant role in "freeing politics and markets in Latin America in the 1990s." Technopols in LAC have been defined as political leaders who are at the highest level of government and political party life, took neoliberal (and democratic) ideas seriously and were able to help transform their nations toward these ideas. Technopols seized a critical moment in LAC history in the early 1980s which paved the way for them to almost fully come into power by the 1990s. That moment was the aftermath of the macroeconomic crises in the early 1980s. Domínguez writes:

> At the moment of economic crisis, there was available an international pool of theoretical and empirical ideas that emphasized the utility of markets; these ideas had become dominant in the industrial countries during the 1970s and the 1980s, precisely when these technopols-in-the-making lived there. These market-oriented international ideas were nested in economics departments, the international financial institutions, and in major private foundations, which fostered and funded the spread of ideas through the think tanks and teams founded by these technopols. The international context was favorable as well because these ideas were supported by the US government, its major allies, and public and private international financial institutions. They "demanded" competence from the economic policy makers of Latin American countries. Technically trained leaders, therefore, would help to generate international and eventually domestic political legitimacy. (1997, 26)

This transformation, of course, became known as the Washington Consensus. Table 6.4 provides a list of each of the FTAs that has been signed between the US and a nation from LAC since the economic crises of the early 1990s. Columns 5 and 6 name the president of the nation at the time of signing an FTA, the individual's political party and whether or not the party and/or president is considered neoliberal by various experts in political science.

The table reveals that the vast majority of nations were neoliberal in nature at the time of signing a trade agreement with the US. However, the Dominican Republic, Uruguay, Jamaica and Chile can be considered left-leaning to various degrees. This shows that while ideas do indeed matter, the forces articulated by liberals and realists must also be at play. As posed earlier, FTAs are not necessarily consistent with neoclassical economics (Panagariya 1999). It might, therefore, appear as a contradiction that neoliberal governments would support FTAs. However, those writing on the

Table 6.4. Does ideology matter when Latin Americans sign trade agreements?

Country	Date of BIT	Date of FTA	Government	Neoliberal?
Nicaragua	2 July 1999	29 May 2008	Violeta Barrios de Chamorro, National Opposition Union (BIT), Enrique Bolaños, Alliance for the Republic (DR-CAFTA)	Y
Dominican Republic		6 August 2008	Hipólito Mejía, Dominican Revolutionary Party	Left-leaning
Honduras	2 July 1999	29 May 2008	Carlos Roberto Reina Idiáquez, Liberal Party of Honduras (BIT), Ricardo Maduro, National Party (DR-CAFTA)	Y
Haiti	14 December 1987		Dr François Duvalier	Y
Costa Rica		29 May 2008	Abel Pacheco, Social Christian Unity Party	Y
Guatemala		29 May 2008	Óscar Berger, Grand National Alliance	Y
Bolivia	18 April 2002		Hugo Banzer, Nationalist Democratic Action	Y
Peru		13 April 2010	Alejandro Toledo, Peru Possible	Y
Trinidad and Tobago	27 September 1998		Patrick Manning, People's National Movement	Y
Uruguay	5 November 2009		Tabare Vazquez, Frente Amplio-Encuentro Progresista	Left-leaning
El Salvador	11 March 2003	29 May 2008	Armando Calderón Sol (BIT), Francisco Guillermo Flores Pérez (DR-CAFTA), Nationalist Republican Alliance	Y
Colombia		23 November 2010	Álvaro Uribe, independent liberal	Y
Grenada	3 May 1990		Herbert Blaize, New National Party	Y
Jamaica	5 February 1998		Percival Noel James Patterson, Jamaican People's National Party	Left-leaning
Panama	28 October 1986	20 December 2010	Ricardo de la Espriella (BIT), Martin Torrijos, Democratic Revolutionary Party (FTA)	Y

(Continued)

Table 6.4. Continued

Country	Date of BIT	Date of FTA	Government	Neoliberal?
Chile		2 January 2008	Ricardo Lagos, Coalition of Parties for Democracy	Left-leaning
Argentina	15 November 1995		Carlos Menem, Justicialist Party	Y
Mexico		18 December 1996	Carlos Salinas de Gortari, Institutional Revolutionary Party	Y

Source: Column 1 (UNCTAD 2007), column 2 (USTR 2007), columns 3 and 4 (Kline and Wiarda 2006).

role of ideas stress that the Washington Consensus has become an *ideology* where the "free" market is dominant. FTAs represent "free trade" and are very much consistent with the ideology of free trade but not necessarily with the economics of free trade.

Technopols put together teams of technocrats that helped form and sustain coalitions with the private sector that helped ensure passage of FTAs. Babb (2001) has shown how neoclassical Mexican economists were fairly powerless relative to their heterodox counterparts. Over the course of one generation Mexico became infamous for being run by US-educated neoclassical economists. Some of the high profile members of this group became presidents and ministers, but Babb shows how this trend became the norm even for lower levels of government bureaucracy as well. Thacker (2000) shows how neoliberal technopols and technocrats shared goals and created coalitions with many large exporting Mexican firms. Indeed in Mexico and across LAC the prospect of an FTA provided an opportunity to push through reforms that were on the technopol agenda anyway but did not have enough momentum to be passed. Packaged as part of a larger deal with the US, leaders were able to argue to their publics that such was the price of the larger agreement which would benefit all.

Dynamic comparative advantage and the collective action problem

Neoclassical trade theory and liberal theories of trade regime formation are static in nature. That is, the "deal" is more often than not a function of the interests, costs and benefits of the negotiating nations at a specific point in time. However, many of the industrial development policies outlined in the previous section are policies to create dynamic comparative advantages. As discussed earlier, if South Korea was to enter into a trade agreement with the US it would have been in the static interests of South Korea to produce and export rice and for the US to produce and export steel – given the relative factor endowments (South Korea had no steel at all in 1970) and resulting coalitions (Amsden 1992b). However, South Korea had a more dynamic view, choosing to forego short-term costs for higher long-term benefits. By 2000 South Korean steel was one of the most formidable in the world. Indeed, the US put protective tariffs on South Korean steel in 2002 under fears that the US industry would be severely damaged by South Korean steel. What's more, by 2007 when South Korea entered an FTA with the US they had to exempt rice from the treaty because it was no longer efficient or competitive relative to the US.

This poses a collective action problem in the short term when a trade agreement is under negotiation (Shadlen 2008). By their very nature many of the industrial policies that developing countries want to maintain the ability to deploy are policies that correct market failures so that firms and general welfare benefits can be created in the future. Thus, the beneficiaries of such policies are either small and weak, or not even yet in existence. In 1970 the steel industry in South Korea did not exist. To take an example from a Latin American country, Brazilian aircraft did not exist before the late 1960s, when Brazil would have been advised to export coffee. Brazil's aircraft industry would not have been able to survive a free trade deal with the US then, but now Embraer is one of the most formidable members of the sector. Previous literature discussing the outcome of FTAs in the literature have argued that the winners of the agreements are diffuse and the losers are concentrated to explain why the FTAs in the hemisphere have been laboring processes (Salazar-Xirinachs 2004). Here the opposite argument is made to explain why in the end the majority of LAC nations have signed agreements with the US: the beneficiaries are highly concentrated in the industries that already have access to the US market in the present and the losers are diffuse across the domestic economy, small and weak, or nonexistent.

Previously published analyses of NAFTA illuminate this assessment. Thacker (2000) showed how Mexico's large exporting firms joined coalitions within the state and in the US to lobby for an agreement. Shadlen (2004) provides an analysis that reveals that smaller domestic firms were not able to get adequate representation at the table. Wise and Pastor (1994) also add that many of the losers were very diffuse and further strapped by information asymmetries at play – many potential actors were simply not aware of the costs. Shadlen (2004) adds, however, that although firms were not privy to the required information about the effects of NAFTA, their representatives in business associations were, and that it is still a puzzle that they did not do more to defend their members.

Summary

This chapter has attempted to bring together and expand upon disparate literatures on the economics and political economy of trade policy in the Americas in order to help us understand the dynamics behind trade politics between the US and LAC. The chapter has three key points. First, that the official modeling estimates regarding the benefits of FTAs between the US and other LAC nations are very small. Second, that the costs of such agreements in terms of lost policy space are significant. Third, that despite the high cost of free trade with the US, LAC nations "trade away" the ability to build dynamic comparative advantages because of a sense of urgency to sign agreements before their neighbors do, because of asymmetric bargaining power between the US and the LAC nations with trade deals, because of the power of ideas and ideology in LAC in support of the Washington Consensus and because nations can't solve the collective action problem whereby the main beneficiaries of dynamic comparative advantage have no "voice" at the negotiating table.

In this chapter, an analysis of the causes of the Latin American FTA paradox is conducted, drawing from the literature on international political economy. It is argued that viewing these agreements as rational win–win bargains has only limited significance. Economic and political power and ideas help explain the dynamics of trade negotiations in LAC. The chapter argues that to some extent the deal on the table offers a constrained set of choices for LAC nations to negotiate about and therefore defines the set of interests of negotiators. There is not much room to maneuver because the US has the power not only to pull out of the negotiations, but to revoke special preferences that many LAC have enjoyed for many years and to deny a nation entry into the largest market in the world. This lends credence to Chang's (2002) thesis that developed countries are "kicking away the ladder" of development enjoyed by the developed countries in earlier times. It also demonstrates that LAC is "trading away that ladder." In the face of US power at the bargaining table, LAC nations lack (formidable) countering interest group pressure because the benefits are concentrated and the costs are disparate – some of these costs (and benefits) fall on future generations and constituents that obviously have no voice in the negotiations. Finally, the leadership of LAC nations were fundamentally engrained in a "free market" mindset. Although instruments by which they pursued such beliefs were at times inconsistent with the free market neoclassical economics that formed the beliefs to begin with, such details were lost in a frenzy to sign trade agreements and similar measures for more than a decade.

Note

1 Political scientists also focus heavily on "realist" and "constructivist" theories to explain trade politics. Often in rich nations, as Mayer (1998) shows, "winning" interests align with political actors concerned with US power (realism) and evoke "symbolism" to help win votes in public (constructivism).

Chapter 7

PUTTING DEVELOPMENT FIRST: TRADE POLICY FOR THE TWENTY-FIRST CENTURY

This book has shown that over the past 30 years emerging market and developing countries have lost a significant amount of policy space to pursue development strategies that have worked in the past for industrialized and developing countries alike. The WTO, and even more so BITs and FTAs, curtail the room to maneuver in the twenty-first century. But each of these deals was a negotiation, implying that nations have traded away this policy space of their own free will. That is true. However this book and the work of others shows that in many cases such "acceptance" was due to asymmetric bargaining power, collective action problems and beyond. Indeed, many of those problems became overturned at the WTO and have prevented the further restriction of policy space for development. This final chapter draws on the rest of the book to put forth some ideas regarding what a world trading system that put development first would look like.

Re-embedding Liberalism

During the postwar period, many developing countries were not yet included in GATT, and, even when they were, they were allowed to play under different rules given that they were not considered much of a threat by the industrialized world. By the 1990s, advanced countries faced competition by some developmental states and asserted a trading system that among other things would place limits on policy space for industrialization and financial stability. This assertion was a victory for industrialized nations seeking to consolidate and expand their comparative advantage through globalization, and became manifest in the formation of the WTO in 1995. By the 2000s, however, a number of developing and emerging market economies engaged in a more "developmental globalization" and gained enough economic and political power that they were able to substantially halt a move toward the further constriction of policy space in the Doha Round. Such a change may be temporary, however. As different waves of developmental globalizers achieve significant levels of development, their own interests shift and their role in blocking full-scale deep integration and the liberalization of trade and industrial policy becomes less steadfast. This raises the important questions for the future of many of the least developing countries.

The seeds of the multilateral trading system were planted in 1944 at the United Nations Monetary and Financial Conference in Bretton Woods, New Hampshire as the world war was dwindling and the Great Depression still loomed large in memory. The Bretton Woods process was very much embedded in what was then referred to as "New Deal" thinking whereby nation-states mandated leeway to improve the welfare of their citizens but to such an extent that it did not unduly impose on the welfare of other nations (Helleiner 2011). Over the past two decades the multilateral trading system has lost sight of that balance, and the WTO could now hardly be seen as a New Deal institution. The current crises that plague the world economy are a challenging opportunity for the WTO to regain that balance.

Preserving and enhancing the multilateral trade regime is of utmost importance in order to foster growth and prosperity in the world economy. Over the past decade, rather than refining the global set of rules and norms at the WTO to that end, negotiations have solely focused on further trade liberalization – despite the fact that the gains from further liberalization are relatively low and the costs can be significant.

The fact that this approach has produced a standstill at the WTO need not be seen as a failure. Rather, the standstill in negotiations for further liberalization is an opportunity for actors in the world trading system to reflect on some of the new challenges in the world trading system and reform the WTO in such a manner that it can become the premiere institution governing the trading system.

The alternative is not optimal: a splintering system of preferential trade agreements (PTAs) that can distort trade, accentuate discrimination and allow private actors to "shop" for the forum that best advances their interest. The world needs a WTO that has accepted norms, enforceable rules and a legitimate forum for the settlement of disputes at the multilateral level. Of all the multilateral institutions the WTO has the most promise to play this role because of its unique one-country/one-vote consensus structure. Can the WTO turn challenge into opportunity?

This short exercise outlines four challenging opportunities facing the WTO. If the WTO is reformed into a more modest, flexible and equitable organization that it can gain the legitimacy and importance hoped for by those who originally recognized the need for a coordinated multilateral trading system in Bretton Woods almost eighty years ago.

Four Challenges for the Multilateral Trade Regime

At least four challenges to the WTO have stopped negotiations for further liberalization in their tracks: the limits of further liberalization, the rise of emerging market developing countries; the food and climate crises; and the instability of the global monetary system. As depression and war challenged the global financial architecture in the 1940s, these trends challenge the WTO today.

1) Shrinking gains and rising costs of liberalization

Trade liberalization has brought significant benefits to the world economy over the past 40 years, yet with real winners and losers. However, the benefits of further liberalization are shrinking, and the costs of deep integration can be significant.

The World Bank's 2005 projections of gains from a "likely" Doha deal were met with much surprise as they showed how little is to be gained from further global trade liberalization (see Ackerman and Gallagher 2008). The World Bank estimated that the global gains from trade liberalization in the year 2015 would be just $96 billion, with only $16 billion going to the developing world. In other words, the developing country benefits represent a one-time increase in income of just 0.16 percent of GDP. This is often misconstrued as an increase in the annual growth rate; it is a one-time increase in GDP. In per capita terms, it amounts to $3.13, or less than a penny per day per capita for those in developing countries.

Studies like these only examine the potential benefits of trade liberalization, while downplaying the costs. Total tariff losses for developing countries under proposed NAMA liberalization were estimated to be as high as $63.4 billion. Many developing countries rely on tariffs for more than one-quarter of their tax revenue. Most models also predict declines in terms of trade for developing countries. In the long run, declining terms of trade undermine developing country efforts to diversify and develop. They can also accentuate balance-of-payments problems in developing countries and deepen the impacts of crises (Wise and Gallagher 2008).

What is more, the gains from adopting industrialized country-style intellectual property rules and financial regulation are also questionable from a development perspective. The World Bank estimates that the amount of South-to-North profit transfers due to patent rents under the WTO's intellectual property rules are $41 billion annually (World Bank 2002). The IMF recently estimated that those nations that liberalized foreign investment in the financial services sector were among those hit hardest during the financial crisis (IMF 2010).

As industrialized nations have become frustrated with lack of integration at the global level, they have pushed PTAs with nations more willing to negotiate. PTAs cause costly trade diversion – perhaps between $6.6 billion and $21.5 billion according to the World Bank (World Bank 2005). What is more, PTAs have nontrade provisions in areas such as intellectual property and financial services that constrain the ability of nations to deploy adequate development policy (as noted in this book's chapter on industrial policy). Finally, many PTAs tip the balance in favor of powerful interests where disputes can be settled with private firms directly filing claims on governments, rather than the state-to-state dispute system that governs the WTO.

2) The rise of the rest

Developing countries have been growing faster than their industrialized counterparts since the turn of the century, and in the aftermath of the global financial crisis the developing world has proved more resilient. This has been due to a hybrid approach to economic development that recognizes the importance of global markets but also realizes that markets need to be embedded in the proper institutions in order to maximize the welfare for national societies. The latter approach has meant that many of the most successful emerging powers – China, Brazil, South Africa and India – have accentuated the role of the state in economic affairs. This has led to a "clash of globalizations" at the WTO (Gallagher 2012).

We could call this variety "developmental globalization." All of these nations have been slow to open their capital accounts to foreign investment. All engage in industrial and state-led innovation policy to some degree. And together these nations form the heads of significant coalitions in global trade talks that have pushed back on industrialized country proposals aimed at making developing countries look more like industrialized economies. They have clout because these nations are fast growing markets to which firms and investors want greater access. They have clout because (in purchasing power parity terms) they lead an emerging market world that has a larger share of GDP in the world economy than Western nations.

The theoretical underpinning of the WTO is to aid nations in maximizing their static comparative advantage. Yet many developing countries have sought to globalize in order to achieve a dynamic comparative advantage (Amsden 2001; Wade 2004a). In many cases that has meant favoring domestic firms or industries over foreign ones, and thus at least in spirit such an approach violates the principle of national treatment. Tariffs in the world economy are relatively low by historical standards and therefore this clash is often not seen to occur in discussions over goods tariffs. What has gone unrecognized by some, though, is that trade treaties are no longer about trade in goods, but rather are about domestic regulations that could be seen as violating the two principles.

As China, India, Brazil, South Africa and others have continued to grow their economies at a significant pace since the turn of the century, they (and their domestic constituents) have fought hard to maintain at minimum the level of policy space they have at the WTO. At the WTO, this meant rejecting the proposals by the developed world to deepen international investment rules, intellectual property rules, government procurement and financial services (the so-called "Singapore Issues" and others).

Moreover, the developing world turned the tables on the narrative of the talks. Whereas past rounds were pitched as the developing world being riddled with protections that are bad for growth and prosperity, the developing world flipped that on its head and accused the North of the same. Almost immediately into the negotiations the developing world made an issue of industrialized country subsidies and tariffs benefiting agricultural producers, and intellectual property rules that prevented developing countries from breaking patents to serve ailing and diseased populations. In effect, this put the developing world on the moral high ground. Rather than getting their Singapore Issues at the 2003 WTO Cancun meetings, the North had to abandon those issues as well as amending the WTO agreements on intellectual property rules to allow for public health exceptions – a key victory for developing countries. Turning away from a "deep integration" agenda, from 2003 on, the negotiations were mostly about market access in agriculture, manufacturing goods and some services. In addition, special attention was to go to the poorest nations in the form of relieving cotton subsidies and "aid for trade" packages.

3) Food and climate crises

Two other major challenges to the trading system are the food and climate crises. Since 2008 the world has entered a new era of highly volatile food prices and a renewed sense of urgency regarding the need to combat climate change. Both these crises require urgent and sometimes drastic attention. It is not clear that the WTO, as currently structured, has the flexibility necessary for the world to combat these challenges. A twenty-first-century WTO would allow nations to respond to contemporary challenges like these.

Since 2007, global food prices have been increasing and volatile, reaching levels not seen since 1990 in 2011. This has adversely affected the livelihoods of many of the world's poorest. These tragic events have triggered a new set of policy responses to ensure food security across the globe. The United Nations Special Rapporteur for the Right to Food (2011) has identified five sets of policies for food security in the twenty-first century:

> (1) Reinvestment in agriculture and general support schemes to small-scale farmers; (2) safety-nets and income-insurance for the urban and rural poor; (3) the establishment of food reserves at national or regional levels to allow governments to cushion the impact of price shocks and to limit volatility of prices for agricultural commodities; (4) orderly market management, including marketing boards and supply management schemes, as another measure to combat volatility; and (5) limiting excessive reliance on international trade in the pursuit of food security. (De Schutter 2011)

A preliminary "compatibility review" of these measures alongside WTO rules conducted by the FAO reveals that these policies are seen as derivations from the WTO rather than as principal objectives of agricultural trade policy.

With respect to the climate crisis, the climate regime is urging the world's nations to rapidly deploy and diffuse technological and process innovation in green technology. A particular emphasis has been on China – which has been told that it needs to deploy such technologies and reduce emissions with little or no financial help from the industrialized world.

China, as an example, has deployed policies to create world-class technologies (such as solar power, where they lowered the global price by 40 percent) but through means that are also not "compatible" with current WTO rules. By 2009, China added more wind power than any other country, including the United States. China already has the largest solar thermal capacity in the world and now leads the world in installed renewable energy capacity. Yet the same industrialized nations that are telling China to deploy clean technology and clean up its act are now taking China to the WTO for violating its rules, particularly rules about subsidies.

What is lost sight of is that the use of climate-altering fossil fuels distorts trade. Subsidizing alternatives can correct those distortions. Oil and coal prices seldom reflect their environmental costs and are thus overproduced. The World Bank's 2010 "World Development Report" reckons that fossil fuel subsidies amount to at least $300 billion per year. If prices reflected true costs, then much less polluting trade would occur and renewable energy would be on a more even playing field.

Subsidies to renewable energy, such as wind power, can help correct the distortions in the energy market and allow the world to climb the learning curve for renewable forms of energy.

4) Instability of the global monetary system

From 1944 to the Tokyo Round, the Bretton Woods agreement ensured exchange rate stability and the swift payment of current account transactions. Exchange rate stability therefore became taken for granted in multilateral trading system. Without stable exchange rates global trade markets are not sent the right signals and global trade transactions will not be a function of factor abundance, productivity or comparative advantage. Since the Tokyo Round the monetary system has become increasingly unstable, and never more so than in the aftermath of the global financial crisis. The multilateral trading system will continue to be jeopardized until the monetary system is reformed.

Exchange rate instability may be the key reason why the Doha Round is permanently stalled, given that key nations such as India, Brazil and South Africa have been socked with exchange rate volatility ever since the crisis began. Take Brazil, for example. Brazil was supportive of the last ditch 2008 deal at the WTO. Brazil's soy and beef industries stood to gain significantly from a WTO deal and many manufacturing firms stood to gain in terms of providing machinery, transport and other inputs. Finally – and this is important – the Brazilian real was relatively undervalued during the first years of the Doha Round. A weak currency is implicitly import-substituting and a subsidy to exports. Thus, Brazilian industry was more open to negotiating. All this changed after the global financial crisis, as Brazil and many other emerging markets have seen their currencies appreciate by more than 40 percent. Brazilian industrialists became staunchly averse to a deal because they lacked competitiveness and saw more concessions as being out of the question. At this point Brazil would never agree to the 2008 deal. According to some calculations Brazil's currency appreciation has effectively amounted to a 25 percent reduction in import tariffs for that country (Thorstensen et al. 2011).

Not only has the misalignment of the monetary and trading system distorted trade flows, but many of the financial regulatory measures that nations deploy to manage the exchange rate are not permitted under the WTO if a nation has listed them under its General Agreement on Trade and Services commitments (Gallagher 2011).

Toward a More Responsive Multilateral Trade Regime

The WTO is poised to become one of the most important institutions in the global financial architecture. Unlike the G-20, the International Monetary Fund and even the United Nations, the WTO has the potential to be the most legitimate of these bodies. The WTO operates on a one-country/one-vote consensus level, whereas the G-20 and IMF decisions are made by the size of a nation's economy and UN decisions can be overridden by the Security Council. Indeed, the WTO has been undersold as a legitimate global economic governance institution.

In general, the WTO should conduct a thorough "compatibility review" regarding the extent to which its principles and rules are compatible with policies for growth, food security, environmental protection and financial stability.

Institutional reform

Rather than focusing on further liberalization the WTO should focus on building its institutional capabilities in order to serve as the global governance structure for world trade. As nations do so they will need to think about their interests further into the future. What we have learned in the past ten years is that some nations that were once LDCs are now among the largest in the world. In a rapidly changing and uncertain world where nations do not know what their place will be, it is in the interest of actors to adhere to the "maximin" principle of attempting to establish rules that will maximize the position of those who are worst off in the current system. There should also be a moratorium on North–South preferential trade agreements. These deals exploit the asymmetric nature of bargaining power between developed and developing nations, divert trade away from nations with true comparative advantages and curtail the ability of developing countries to deploy effective policies for development.

Food

The WTO should take seriously the proposals by many African nations to tame highly concentrated global commodities markets, dominated by agribusinesses that suck most of the value out of these value chains. Rich nations should also grant poorer countries extensive rights to exempt staples of their local economy such as corn, rice and wheat – so-called "special products" – from tariff cuts, and allow them to raise duties when imports surge. Moreover, policies to create food reserves, marketing boards and supply management schemes should be seen as advancing world trade, not distorting it.

Climate

The WTO needs to leave ample room for the transfer of clean technology to developing countries. Otherwise the diffusion of new technologies and mitigation strategies will get bogged down in global rules over intellectual property, investment and goods trade. There is room for creative thinking whereby specific collaborative efforts between, say, the United States and China could be granted immunity for a specific period under the WTO in order to meet certain emissions and technology targets – in a manner analogous to, but much broader than, the Article 8 exceptions to the subsidies agreement to the WTO.

Finance

National and global financial authorities will be the ones to determine what a new global monetary system looks like in the wake of the financial crisis. In the meantime, the WTO should conduct a thorough review of the extent to which its principles and rules are compatible with various measures that nations can deploy to prevent and mitigate financial crises. In the absence of a stable monetary system, nations will have to resort to measures such as capital account regulations that at present seem to be incompatible with the WTO.

Upon the reflection outlined here, the WTO will become a more modest global institution, but one with more legitimacy and a stronger mandate. More importantly, it will allow nations the flexibility to improve and maintain the welfare of their citizens at present and in future generations – and to an extent, ensure that the actions of individual nations do not unduly impose on the welfare of other nations – as the founders of the global economic architecture had hoped for in 1944.

This book has shown that the 2000s may have been a unique moment of "equity-enhancing multilateralism," whereby the WTO was able to yield pluralistic outcomes that allowed each member to pursue its own development policies within the existing set of rules at the WTO. This was due to the fact that the distribution of economic power was dispersed across income classes that had a variety of views of successful globalization, with many key and economically powerful emerging market nations using a one-country/one-vote consensus system to maintain the status quo. Given that we do not really know the exact recipe for growth and development, and indeed that history has shown that a wide variety of approaches can work, this could be seen in a normative sense as a positive outcome.

However parsimonious this model may seem, it is sure to be unstable. History has shown that domestic interests, regardless of the level of development, play a large part in setting the negotiating position of nations. Therefore, one cannot expect that nations which used a particular set of policies at one stage of development will be favorable to allowing other nations to have that same flexibility over time. Indeed, history points in the opposite direction. Europe, the US and Japan all pushed for a very shallow GATT in its early years in order to expand domestic capabilities. When those capabilities became global and nations become capital exporters, their interests changed. South Korea is another example. South Korea was a quintessential developmental state but was a leader in pushing the Singapore Issues in Cancun. Now that South Korea is a capital exporter, its multinational firms do not want to be subject to capital controls and performance requirements, even if it was those very policies that played a role in bringing those firms to multinational status. We have begun to see this with China as well. While it has stayed in step with Brazil, India and South Africa for most of the WTO round, its bilateral investment treaties have increasingly begun to look more and more like developed world treaties.

From a policy perspective, then, when the larger emerging market and developing countries begin to become capital exporters, they, too, may have more in common with the West. Equal rules for unequal members may spell unequal rules in reality. It may just be that ideas, the WTO's institutional structure and the international balance of market power aligned in a unique way to provide policy space for developing countries during the Doha Round. This particular mix of independent variables may be impossible to replicate over time, even if we could specifically quantify what the relative importance of each factor was. What is more likely is that those nations that have drawn a line in the sand now will want to erase that line as they export to poorer countries. This could be problematic in terms of the longer-run availability of policy space for the least developed countries (LDCs), because after the larger nations that have been discussed here, there are few large economies left – especially economies that have not already signed a PTA with the US or EU. Moreover, there is a majority of emerging market and developing countries that does not see virtue in developmental globalization. They rush to sign BITs and PTAs with industrialized countries. It is just this smaller number of countries with large economies that have sway at the WTO and largely do not engage in BITs and FTAs with developed countries. When that group changes its interests, there will be a whole patchwork regime greeting them with open arms. So the beginning of the twenty-first century may have been a moment of victory for larger developmental globalizers, but it is not clear that such an era will be permanent. Where will that leave the smaller and still less-developed countries? How will they carve out the policy space that they need to propel their development?

REFERENCES

Abbott, Frederick M. 2004. "The Doha Declaration on the TRIPS Agreement and Public Health and the Contradictory Trend in Bilateral and Regional Free Trade Agreements." Quaker United Nations Office Occasional Paper.

Ackerman, Frank. 2005. "The Shrinking Gains from Trade: A Critical Assessment of Doha Round Projections." Working paper 05–06, Global Development and Environment Institute, Tufts University.

Ackerman, Frank and Kevin P. Gallagher. 2008. "The Shrinking Gains from Global Trade Liberalization in Computable General Equilibrium Models: A Critical Assessment." *International Journal of Political Economy* 37, no. 1: 50–77.

ActionAid, Christian Aid and Oxfam. 2008. "EU FTA Manual, Briefing 4: The EU's Approach to Free Trade Agreements: Services." Online: http://www.oxfam.org.uk/resources/policy/trade/downloads/fta4_services.pdf (accessed 12 September 2012).

Aggarwal, Vinod, Ralph Espach and Joseph Tulchin. 2004. *The Strategic Dynamics of Latin American Trade.* Palo Alto: Stanford University Press.

Aguayo, Francisco and Kevin P. Gallagher. 2009. "Subsidizing Sustainable Development in the WTO." *Journal of World Investment and Trade* 10, no. 1: 1–24.

Akyüz, Yilmaz. 2005. *The WTO Negotiations on Industrial Tariffs: What is at Stake for Developing Countries?* Geneva: Third World Network.

Alfaro, Laura. 2004. "Capital Controls: A Political Economy Approach." *Review of International Economics* 12, no. 4: 571–90.

Amsden, Alice. 1992a. "A Theory of Government Intervention in Late Industrialization." In *State and Market in Development: Synergy or Rivalry?*, edited by Louis Putterman and Dietrich Rueschmeyer. Boulder: Lynne Rienner Publishers. 53–84.

———. 1992b. *Asia's Next Giant: South Korea and Late Industrialization.* Cambridge: Cambridge University Press.

———. 2001. *The Rise of "The Rest": Challenges to the West from Late-Industrializing Economies.* Oxford: Oxford University Press.

———. 2003. "Industrialization under new WTO law." In *Trade and Development: Directions for the 21st Century*, edited by John Toye. Cheltenham: Edward Elgar. 82–99.

———. 2005. "Promoting Industry under WTO Law." In *Putting Development First: The Importance of Policy Space in the WTO and IFIs*, edited by Kevin P. Gallagher. London: Zed Books. 216–32.

———. 2012. "The 'New' Industrial Policy: Securing the Home Market with Subterfuge and SMEs." In *New Visions for Market Governance: Crisis and Renewal*, edited by Kate Macdonald, Shelley Marshall and Sanjay Pinto. London: Routledge. 148–60.

Anderson, Kym and William Martin, eds. 2005. *Agricultural Trade Reform and the Doha Development Agenda.* Washington DC: World Bank.

Anderson, Kym, William Martin and Dominique van der Mensbrugghe. 2006. "Global Impacts of the Doha Scenarios on Poverty." In *Poverty and the WTO: Impacts of the Doha Development Agenda*, edited by Thomas W. Hertel and L. Alan Winters. Washington DC: World Bank. 497–528.

Anderson, Sarah. 2009. "U.S.–China Bilateral Investment Treaty Negotiations: Fact Sheet." Institute for Policy Studies.

_____. 2009. "Policy Handcuffs in the Financial Crisis: How U.S. Trade and Investment Policies Limit Government Power to Control Capital Flows." Institute for Policy Studies, 9 February.

Arrow, Kenneth J. 1962. "The Economic Implications of Learning by Doing." *Review of Economic Studies* 29, no. 3: 155–73.

Babb, Sarah. 2001. *Managing Mexico: Economists from Nationalism to Neoliberalism.* Princeton: Princeton University Press.

Balassa, Bela. 1978. "Export Incentives and Export Performance in Developing Countries: A Comparative Analysis." *Review of World Economics* 114, no. 1: 24–61.

Barro, Robert. 1997. *The Determinants of Economic Growth: A Cross-Country Empirical Study.* Cambridge, MA: MIT Press.

Bhagwati, Jagdish. 2005. "From Seattle to Hong Kong." *Foreign Affairs*, Special WTO Edition. Online: http://www.foreignaffairs.com/articles/61211/jagdish-bhagwati/from-seattle-to-hong-kong (accessed 1 May 2013).

Bhala, Raj. 2003. "World Agricultural Trade in Purgatory: The Uruguay Round Agriculture Agreement and its Implications for the DOHA Round." *North Dakota Law Review* 79: 691–830.

Block, Fred. 2008. "Swimming Against the Current: The Rise of a Hidden Developmental State in the United States." *Politics & Society* 36, no. 2: 169–206.

Blustein, Paul. 2001. *The Chastening: Inside the Crisis that Rocked the Global Financial System and Humbled the IMF.* New York: PublicAffairs.

_____. 2005. *And the Money Kept Rolling In (And Out): Wall Street, the IMF, and the Bankrupting of Argentina.* New York: PublicAffairs.

Bouet, Antoine. 2006. "How Much Will Trade Liberalization Help the Poor?: Comparing Global Trade Models." International Food Policy Research Institute (IFPRI) Research Brief no. 5.

Breslin, Shaun. 2007. *China and the Global Political Economy.* Basingstoke: Palgrave Macmillan.

Brown, Drusilla K., Kozo Kiyota and Robert M. Stern. 2005. "Computational Analysis of the Free Trade Area of the Americas (FTAA)." *North American Journal of Economics and Finance* 16, no. 2: 153–85.

Burke-White, William. 2008. "The Argentine Financial Crisis: State Liability under BITs and the Legitimacy of the ICSID System." *Asian Journal of WTO and International Health Law and Policy* 199: 1–26.

Burton, John. 1983. *Picking Losers…?: The Political Economy of Industrial Policy.* London: Institute of Economic Affairs.

Cadot, Olivier, Antoni Estevadeordal and Akiko Suwa-Eisenmann. 2005. "Rules of Origin as Export Subsidies." CEPR Discussion Paper 4999.

Caliari, Aldo. 2009. "Risk Associated with Trends in the Treatment of Sovereign Debt in Bilateral Trade and Investment Treaties." In *Compendium on Debt Sustainability and Development.* Geneva: UNCTAD. 211–18.

Calvo, Guillermo. 2009. "The New Bretton Woods Agreement." In *What G20 Leaders Must Do to Stabilise our Economy and Fix the Financial System*, edited by Barry Eichengreen and Richard Baldwin. London: VoxEU.

CAN (The Commission of the Cartagena Agreement). 1998. "Decision 439: General Framework of Principles and Rules and for Liberalizing the Trade in Services in the Andean Community." *Andean Community of Nations*, 11 June. Online: http://www.comunidadandina.org/ingles/normativa/D439e.htm (accessed 12 September 2012).

_____. 1991a. "Decisión 292: Régimen Uniforme para Empresas Multinacionales Andinas." Andean Community of Nations, 21 March. Online: http://www.sice.oas.org/trade/junac/decisiones/Dec292s.asp (accessed 12 September 2012).

_____. 1991b. "Decisión 291: Régimen Común de Tratamiento a los Capitales Extranjeros y sobre Marcas, Patentes, Licencias y Regalías." Andean Community of Nations, 21 March. Online: http://www.wipo.int/clea/docs_new/pdf/es/can/can009es.pdf (accessed 12 September 2012).

_____. 2000. "Decision 486: Common Intellectual Property Regime." Andean Community of Nations, 14 September. Online: http://www.comunidadandina.org/ingles/normativa/D486e.htm (accessed 12 September 2012).

_____. 2003. "Decision 563: Official Codified Text of the Andean Subregional Integration Agreement (Cartagena Agreement)." Andean Community of Nations, 25 June. Online: http://www.comunidadandina.org/ingles/normativa/D563e.htm (accessed 11 September 2012).

Canada Foreign Affairs and International Trade. 2010. *Canada–Colombia Free Trade Agreement.* Online: http://www.international.gc.ca/trade-agreements-accords-commerciaux/agr-acc/colombia-colombie/can-colombia-toc-tdm-can-colombie.aspx (accessed 27 March 2013).

Carpenter, Theresa. 2009. "A Historical Perspective on Regionalism." In *Multilateralizing Regionalism: Challenges for the Global Trading System*, edited by Richard Baldwin and Patrick Low. Geneva: The Graduate Institute. 13–27.

Carrizosa, Mauricio, Aaditya Mattoo, Carsten Fink, David Tarr, Glenn W. Harrison, Thomas Rutherford and Angelo Gurgel. 2004. *Brazil-Trade Policies to Improve Efficiency, Increase Growth and Reduce Poverty.* Washington DC: World Bank.

Caves, Richard, Jeffrey A. Frankel and Ronald Jones. 2007. *World Trade and Payments: An Introduction.* London: Pearson.

Center for Policy Alternatives. 2007. *NAFTA Chapter-11 Investor-State Disputes.* Canada: CPR.

Chang, Ha-Joon. 2002. *Kicking Away the Ladder: Development Strategy in Historical Perspective.* London: Anthem Press.

Chaudhuri, Shubham, Pinelopi K. Goldberg and Panle Jia. 2004. "Estimating the Effects of Global Patent Protection in Pharmaceuticals: A Case Study of Quinolones in India." NBER Working Paper No. 10159.

China–Chile. 2005. Free Trade Agreement between the Government of the People's Republic of China and the Government of the Republic of Chile, 18 November. Online: http://wits.worldbank.org/GPTAD/PDF/archive/Chile-china.pdf (accessed 11 September 2012).

Cohen, Benjamin. 2007. *Global Monetary Governance.* London: Routledge.

Cornford, Andrew. 2004. "The WTO Negotiations on Financial Services: Current Issues and Future Directions." UNCTAD Discussion Papers No. 172.

Correa, Carlos M. and Nagesh Kumar. 2003. *Protecting Foreign Investment: Implications of a WTO Regime and Policy Options.* New Delhi: Academic Foundation.

CPA (Canadian Center for Policy Alternatives). 2007. NAFTA, chapter 11: "Investor State Disputes." Ottawa: Canadian Center for Policy Alternatives.

Cross, Karen. 2006. "Arbitration as a Means of Resolving Sovereign Debt Disputes." *American Review of International Arbitration* 17, no. 3: 335–82.

Damill, Mario, Roberto Frenkel and Martín Rapetti. 2010. "The Argentinean Debt: History, Default and Restructuring." In *Overcoming Developing Country Debt Crises*, edited by Barry Herman, José Antonio Ocampo and Shari Spiegel. New York: Oxford University Press. 179–228.

de Córdoba, Santiago Fernández, Sam Laird and David Vanzetti. 2005. "Trick or Treat? Development Opportunities and Challenges in the WTO Negotiations on Industrial Tariffs." *World Economy* 28, no. 10: 1375–1400.

de Córdoba, Santiago Fernández and David Vanzetti. 2006. "Now What? Searching for a Solution to the WTO Industrial Tariff Negotiations." In *Coping with Trade Reforms: A Developing-Country Perspective on the WTO Industrial Tariff Negotiations*, edited by Sam Laird and Santiago Fernandez de Córdoba. Basingstoke: Palgrave Macmillan.

DeRosa, Dean A. and John P. Gilbert. 2004. "Technical Appendix: Quantitative Estimates of the Economic Impacts of US Bilateral Free Trade Agreements." In *Free Trade Agreements: US Strategies and Priorities*, edited by Jeffrey J. Schott. Washington DC: Institute for International Economics. 383–417.

De Schutter, Olivier. 2011. *The World Trade Organization and the Post-Global Food Crisis Agenda: Putting Food Security First in the International Trade System*. United Nations Food and Agriculture Organization Activity Report.

Devlin, Robert and Antoni Estevadeordal. 2004. "Trade and Cooperation: A Regional Public Goods Approach." In *Regional Public Goods: From Theory to Practice*, edited by Antoni Estevadeordal, Brian Frantz and Tam Robert Nguyen. Washington DC: Inter-American Development Bank. 155–80.

Dhillon, Amrita, Javier García Fronti, Sayantan Ghosal and Marcus Miller. 2006. "Bargaining and Sustainability: The Argentine Debt Swap of 2005." *World Economy* 29, no. 4: 377–98.

Domínguez, Jorge. 1997. *Technopols: Freeing Politics and Markets in Latin America in the 1990s*. University Park: Penn State University Press.

DR–CAFTA. 2004. Dominican Republic–Central America–United States Free Trade Agreement. Office of the United States Trade Representative (USTR), 5 August. Online: http://www.ustr.gov/trade-agreements/free-trade-agreements/cafta-dr-dominican-republic-central-america-fta/final-text (accessed 11 September 2012).

DSU. 1994. Understanding on Rules and Procedures Governing the Settlement of Disputes, 15 April, Marrakesh Agreement Establishing the World Trade Organization, Annex 2, Legal Instruments – Results of the Uruguay Round, 33 I.L.M. 1125.

Durán Lima, José E., Carlos J. de Miguel and Andrés R. Schuschny. 2007. "Trade Agreements by Colombia, Ecuador and Peru with the United States: Effects on Trade, Production and Welfare." *CEPAL Review* 91.

Edsall, Rachel D. 2006. "Indirect Expropriation under NAFTA and DR–CAFTA: Potential Inconsistencies in the Treatment of State Public Welfare Regulations." *Boston University Law Review* 86: 931–62.

Eichengreen, Barry. 2003. "Restructuring Sovereign Debt." *Journal of Economic Perspectives* 17, no. 4: 75–98.

Eichengreen, Barry and Ashoka Mody. 2003. "Is Aggregation a Problem for Sovereign Debt Restructuring?" *American Economic Review* 93, no. 2: 80–84.

Eichengreen, Barry, Ricardo Hausmann and Ugo Panizza. 2005. "The Pain of Original Sin." In *Other People's Money: Debt Denomination and Financial Instability in Emerging Market Economies*, edited by Barry Eichengreen and Ricardo Hausmann. Chicago: Chicago University Press. 13–47.

Epstein, Gerald. 2005. *Capital Flight and Capital Controls in Developing Countries*. Northampton: Edward Elgar.

Epstein, Gerald, Ilene Grabel and Jomo K. S. 2008. "Capital Management Techniques in Developing Countries: Managing Capital Flows in Malaysia, India, and China." In *Capital Market Liberalization and Development*, edited by José Antonio Ocampo and Joseph E. Stiglitz. Oxford: Oxford University Press. 139–69.

EU–CARIFORUM. 2008. Economic Partnership Agreement between the CARIFORUM States, of the One Part, and the European Community and its Member States, of the Other Part, 30 October, O.J. (L 289/I) 3.

EU–Chile. 2002. Agreement Establishing an Association between the European Community and its Member States, of one part, and the Republic of Chile, of the other part, 11 November, O.J. (L 352).

EU–Mexico. 2000. Decision No. 2/2000 of the EC–Mexico Joint Council of 23 March – Joint Declarations Title VI, O.J. (L 157) 10.

EU–Mexico. 2001. Decision No. 2/2001 of the EU–Mexico Joint Council of 27 Feb. 2001 – Implementing Articles 6, 9, 12(2)(b) and 50 of the Economic Partnership, Political Coordination and Cooperation Agreement, 27 February, O.J. (L 70) 7.

EU–South Africa. 1999. Agreement on Trade, Development and Cooperation between the European Community and its Member States, of the one part, and the Republic of South Africa, of the other part, 4 December, O.J. (L 311) 3.

EU–Tunisia. 1998. Euro–Mediterranean Agreement Establishing an Association between the European Communities and their Member States, of the one part, and the Republic of Tunisia, of the other part, 30 March, O.J. (L 097) 2.

Evans, Peter B. 1995. *Embedded Autonomy: States and Industrial Transformation*. Princeton: Princeton University Press.

Evenett, Simon J. and Michael Meier. 2008. "An Interim Assessment of the US Trade Policy of 'Competitive Liberalization.'" *World Economy* 31, no. 1: 31–66.

Fiorentino, Roberto V., Jo-Ann Crawford and Christelle Toqueboeuf. 2009. "The Landscape of Regional Trade Agreements and WTO Surveillance." In *Multilateralizing Regionalism: Challenges for the Global Trading System*, edited by Richard Baldwin and Patrick Low. Geneva: The Graduate Institute. 28–79.

Francois, Joseph, Hans van Meijl and Frank van Tongeren. 2003. "Trade Liberalization and Developing Countries under the Doha Round." Tinbergen Institute Discussion Paper 2003-060/2.

Friedman, Milton. 1962. *Capitalism and Freedom*. Chicago: University of Chicago Press.

Gallagher, Kevin P., ed. 2005. *Putting Development First: The Importance of Policy Space in the WTO and IFIs*. London: Zed Books.

_____. 2008a. "Trading Away the Ladder?: Trade Politics and Economic Development in the Americas." *New Political Economy* 13: 37–59.

_____. 2008b. "Understanding Developing Country Resistance to the Doha Round." *Review of International Political Economy* 15, no. 1: 62–85.

_____. 2011. "Losing Control: Policy Space for Capital Controls in Trade and Investment Agreements." *Development Policy Review* 29, no. 4: 387–413.

_____. 2012. "Developmental Globalization and Equity-Enhancing Multilateralism." In *Re-Embedding the Market*, edited by Sanjay Pinto. London: Routledge.

Gallagher, Kevin P. and Rachel D. Thrasher. 2010. "21st Century Trade Agreements: Implications for Development Sovereignty." *Denver Journal of International Law and Policy* 38: 313–50.

GATS (General Agreement on Trade in Services). 1994. Marrakesh Agreement Establishing the World Trade Organization, Annex 1B, Legal Instruments – Results of the Uruguay Round, 15 April. 33 I.L.M. 1125.

GATT (General Agreement on Tariffs and Trade). 1947. 30 October, 61 Stat. A-11, 55 U.N.T.S. 194.

———. 1979. Differential and More Favorable Treatment: Reciprocity and Fuller Participation of Developing Countries, Decision of 28 November (L/4903). GATT Tokyo Round Document LT/TR/D/1. Online: http://www.wto.org/english/docs_e/legal_e/tokyo_enabling_e.pdf (accessed 12 September 2012).

———. 1994. Final Act Embodying the Results of the Uruguay Round of Multilateral Trade Negotiations, 15 April. 33 I.L.M. 1125.

Gelpern, Anna and Brad Setser. 2004. "Domestic and External Debt: The Doomed Quest for Equal Treatment." *Georgetown Journal of International Law* 35, no. 4: 795–814.

Gerschenkron, Alexander. 1966. *Economic Backwardness in Historical Perspective*. Cambridge, MA: Belknap Press.

Gilpin, Robert. 1987. *The Political Economy of International Relations*. Princeton: Princeton University Press.

Giordano, Paolo. 2010. "Assessing Public Policies in Latin America." Washington DC: Inter-American Development Bank.

Global Sovereign Credit Risk Report, Q2 2010, July 2010.

Goldstein, Judith and Robert Keohane. 1993. "Ideas and Foreign Policy: An Analytical Framework." In *Ideas and Foreign Policy: Beliefs, Institutions, and Political Change*, edited by Judith Goldstein and Robert Keohane. Ithaca: Cornell University Press. 3–30.

Gorbunov, Sergei. 2010. "The Russian Federation: From Financial Pariah to Star Reformer." In *Overcoming Developing Country Debt Crises*, edited by Barry Herman, José Antonio Ocampo and Shari Spiegel. New York: Oxford University Press. 161–78.

Grabel, Ilene. 2003. "Averting Crisis?: Assessing Measures to Manage Financial Integration in Emerging Economies." *Cambridge Journal of Economics* 27, no. 3: 317–36.

Grossman, Gene N. and Elhanan Helpman. 1991. *Innovation and Growth in the Global Economy*. Cambridge, MA: MIT Press.

Gruber, Lloyd. 2001. "Power Politics and the Free Trade Bandwagon." *Comparative Political Studies* 34, no. 7: 730–41.

Hagan, Sean. 2000. *Transfer of Funds: UNCTAD Series on Issues in International Investment Agreements*. Geneva: United Nations Conference on Trade and Development.

———. 2005. "Designing a Legal Framework to Restructure Sovereign Debt." *Georgetown Journal of International Law* 36, no. 2: 390–92.

Hall, Peter A. and David Soskice. 2001. "An Introduction to Varieties of Capitalism." In *Varieties of Capitilism: The Institutional Foundations of Comparative Advantage*, edited by Peter A. Hall and David Soskice. Oxford: Oxford University Press. 1–68.

Haslam, P. Alexander. 2004. "BITing Back: Bilateral Investment Treaties and the Struggle to Define an Investment Regime for the Americas." *Policy and Society* 24, no. 3: 91–112.

Helleiner, Eric. 1994. *States and the Reemergence of Global Finance: From Bretton Woods to the 1990s*. Ithaca: Cornell University Press.

———. 2008. "The Mystery of the Missing Sovereign Debt Restructuring Mechanism." *Contributions to Political Economy* 27, no. 1: 91–113.

———. 2009. "Filling a Hole in Global Financial Governance?: The Politics of Regulating Sovereign Debt Restructuring." In *The Politics of Global Regulation*, edited by Walter Mattli and Ngaire Woods. Princeton: Princeton University Press. 89–120.

———. 2011. "Contemporary Reform of Global Financial Governance: Implications of and Lessons from the Past." In *Reforming the International Financial System for Development*, edited by Jomo Kwame Sundaram. New York: Columbia University Press. 1–24.

Herman, Barry, José Antonio Ocampo and Shari Spiegel, eds. 2010. *Overcoming Developing Country Debt Crises*. New York: Oxford University Press.

Hertel, Thomas W. and Roman Kenney. 2006. "What's at Stake?: The Relative Importance of Import Barriers, Export Subsidies and Domestic Support." In *Agriculture Trade Reform and the Doha Development Agenda*, edited by Kym Anderson and William Martin. Washington DC: World Bank. 37–62.

Hilaire, Alvin and Yongzheng Yang. 2004. "The United States and the New Regionalism." IMF Working Paper 03/206. Washington DC; International Monetary Fund.

Hirschman, Albert. 1945. *National Power and the Structure of Foreign Trade:Publications of the Bureau of Business and Economic Research, University of California*. Berkeley: University of California Press.

_____. 1958. *The Strategy of Economic Development*. New Haven: Yale University Press.

Hoekman, Bernard and Michel Kostecki. 2000. *The Political Economy of the World Trading System*. New York: Oxford University Press.

Hornbeck, Jeff. 2003. "The U.S.–Chile Free Trade Agreement: Economic and Trade Policy Issues." CRS Report for Congress, Washington DC.

_____. 2010. *Argentina's Defaulted Sovereign Debt: Dealing with the "Holdouts."* United States Congressional Research Service, July.

ICSID (International Centre for the Settlement of Investment Disputes). 2011. "Abaclat and others versus Argentina: Decision on Jurisdiction and Admissibility." ICSID Case No. ARB/07/5.

IISD (International Institute for Sustainable Development). 2005. "IISD Model International Agreement on Investment." Winnipeg: IISD.

ILO (International Labour Organization). 2008. "Report on the InFocus Initiative on export Processing Zones (EPZs): Latest Trends and Policy Developments in EPZs." International Labour Office Governing Body, GB.301/ESP/5.18 18 February. Online: http://www.ilo.org/wcmsp5/groups/public/---ed_norm/---relconf/documents/meetingdocument/wcms_090223.pdf (accessed 12 September 2012).

ILP. 1994. Agreement on Import Licensing Procedures, 15 April. Marrakesh Agreement Establishing the World Trade Organization, Annex 1A, Legal Instruments – Results of the Uruguay Round, 33 I.L.M. 1125.

Imbs, Jean and Romain Wacziarg. 2003. "Stages of Diversification." *American Economic Review* 93, no. 1: 63–86.

IMF (International Monetary Fund). 2002. *Sovereign Debt Restructuring Mechanism Further Considerations*. Washington DC: International Monetary Fund.

_____. 2009a. *World Economic Outlook Database*, April. Online: http://www.imf.org/external/pubs/ft/weo/data/changes.htm (accessed 13 April 2013).

_____. 2009b. "Annual Report on Exchange Arrangements and Exchange Restrictions." Washington DC: International Monetary Fund.

_____. 2010. "Capital Inflows: The Role of Controls." IMF Staff Position Notes. Washington DC: International Monetary Fund.

Johnson, Chalmers. 1982. *MITI and the Japanese Miracle: The Growth of Industrial Policy, 1925–1975*. Palo Alto: Stanford University Press.

Jyaraman, Tiru K. and Baljeet Singh. 2007. "Foreign Direct Investment and Employment Creation in Pacific Island Countries: An Empirical Study of Fiji." Asia-Pacific Research and Training Network on Trade, Working Paper Series No. 35.

Key, Sydney. 2003. *The Doha Round and Financial Services Negotiations*. Washington DC: AEI Press.

Kim, Linsu and Richard Nelson, eds. 2000. *Technology, Learning, and Innovation: Experiences of Newly Industrializing Economies*. Cambridge: Cambridge University Press.

Kireyev, Alexei. 2002. "Liberalization of Trade in Financial Services and Financial Sector: Stability Analytical Approach." IMF Working Paper No. 02/138. Washington DC: International Monetary Fund.

Kline, Harvey and Howard Wiarda. 2006. *Latin American Politics and Development*. Boulder: Westview Press.

Kolo, Abba and Thomas Wälde. 2009. "Economic Crises, Capital Transfer Restrictions, and Investor Protection under Modern Investment Treaties." *Capital Markets Law Journal* 3, no. 2: 154–85.

Kose, M. Ayhan, Eswar S. Prasad and Ashley D. Taylor. 2009. "Thresholds on the Process of International Financial Integration." NBER Working Paper No. 14916.

Kowalczyk, Carsten. 1989. "Trade Negotiations and World Welfare." *American Economic Review* 79: 552–9.

_____. 2002. "Reforming Tariffs and Subsidies in International Trade." *Pacific Economic Review* 7, no. 2: 552–9.

Kowalczyk, Carsten and Ronald Wonnacott. 1992. "Hubs and Spokes, and Free Trade in the Americas." NBER Working Paper No. 4198.

Krueger, Anne. 1996. *The Political Economy of Trade Protection:A National Bureau of Economic Research Project Report*. Chicago: University of Chicago Press.

_____. 2002. *A New Approach to Sovereign Debt Restructuring*. Washington DC: International Monetary Fund.

Krugman, Paul. 1979. "A Model of Innovation, Technology Transfer, and the World Distribution of Income." *Journal of Political Economy* 87, no. 2: 253–66.

_____. 1991. "History versus Expectations." *Quarterly Journal of Economics* 106, no. 2: 651–67.

_____. 1995. *Development, Geography, and Economic Theory*. Cambridge, MA: MIT Press.

Kumar, Nagesh and Kevin P. Gallagher. 2007. "Relevance of 'Policy Space' for Development: Implications for Multilateral Trade Negotiations." Research and Information System for Developing Countries, Discussion Paper No. 120.

Lall, Sanjaya. 2000. "Technological Change and Industrialization in the Asian Newly Industrializing Economies: Achievements and Challenges." In *Technology, Learning, and Innovation: Experiences of Newly Industrializing Economies*, edited by Linsu Kim and Richard Nelson. Cambridge: Cambridge University Press. 13–68.

_____. 2005. "Rethinking Industrial Strategy: The Role of the State in the Face of Globalization." In *Putting Development First: The Importance of Policy Space in the WTO and IFIs*, edited by Kevin P. Gallagher. London: Zed Books. 33–68.

Lawrence, Robert Z. 1996. *Regionalism, Multilateralism, and Deeper Integration: Integrating National Economies*. Washington DC: Brookings Institution.

Lipsey, R. G. and Kelvin Lancaster. 1956. "The General Theory of Second Best." *Review of Economic Studies* 24, no. 1: 11–32.

Lucas, Robert. 1988. "On the Mechanisms of Economic Development." *Journal of Monetary Economics* 22: 3–42.

Magud, Nicolas and Carmen M. Reinhart. 2006. "Capital Controls: An Evaluation." NBER Working Paper No. 11973.

Marconini, Mario. 2006. "Regional Trade Agreements and Their Impact on Services Trade." ICTSD Policy Paper on Trade in Services and Sustainable Development (draft).

Mayer, Frederick W. 1998. *Interpreting NAFTA: The Science and Art of Political Analysis*. New York: Columbia University Press.

Mayer, Jörg. 2009. "Policy Space: What, for What, and Where?" *Development Policy Review* 27, no. 4: 373–95.

Melo, Andrew. 2001. "Industrial Policy in Latin America and the Caribbean at the Turn of the Century." Research Department Working Paper 459. Washington DC: Inter-American Development Bank.

MERCOSUR. 1991a. Treaty Establishing a Common Market between the Argentine Republic, the Federal Republic of Brazil, the Republic of Paraguay and the Eastern Republic of Uruguay Annex I, 26 March. 30 I.L.M. 1041.

———. 1991b. Treaty of Asunción, 26 March. 30 I.L.M. 1041.

———. 1994. Protocol of Colonia for the Promotion and Reciprocal Protection of Investments in MERCOSUR, 17 January. Securities and Exchange Commission of Brazil. Online: http://www.cvm.gov.br/port/relinter/ingles/mercosul/coloni-e.asp (accessed 11 September 2012).

———. 1995. Protocol on Harmonization of Norms on Intellectual Property in MERCOSUR in Matters of Trademarks, Indications of Source and Appellations of Origin, 5 August. 2145 U.N.T.S. 460.

———. 1997. Montevideo Protocol on Trade in Services of MERCOSUR, 15 December. Securities and Exchange Commission of Brazil. Online: http://www.cvm.gov.br/port/relinter/ingles/mercosul/montv-e.asp (accessed 11 September 2012).

Michaud, Michael (Representative). 2009. "Amendment to HR 4173: Certain Requirements Relating to Trade Agreement." Washington DC: United States House of Representatives.

Minsky, Hyman. 1986. *Stabilizing an Unstable Economy*. New Haven: Yale University Press.

Moe, Terry. 2005. "Power and Political Institutions." *Perspectives on Politics* 3, no. 2: 215–33.

Murphy, Kevin M., Andrei Shleifer and Robert W. Vishny. 1989. "Industrialization and the Big Push." *Journal of Political Economy* 97, no. 5: 1003–26.

Musungu, Sisule F., Susan Villanueva and Roxanna Blasetti. 2004. *Utilizing TRIPS Flexibilities for Public Health Protection through South-South Regional Frameworks*. Geneva: South Centre.

NAFTA (North American Free Trade Agreement). 1993. May, 32 I.L.M. 605.

Narlikar, Amrita. 2004. "Developing Countries and the WTO." In *Trade Politics: International, Domestic, and Regional Perspectives*, 2nd ed., edited by Brian Hocking and Steve McGuire. London: Routledge.

Narlikar, Amrita and Diana Tussie. 2004. "The G20 at the Cancun Ministerial: Developing Countries and their Evolving Coalitions in the WTO." *World Economy* 27, no. 7: 947–66.

Nelson, Richard R. and Sidney G. Winter. 1982. *An Evolutionary Theory of Economic Change*. Cambridge, MA: Harvard College.

Newcombe, Andrew and Lluís Paradell. 2009. *Law and Practice of Investment Treaties – Standards of Treatment*. The Hague: Kluwer Law International.

Noland, Marcus and Howard Pack. 2003. *Industrial Policy in an Era of Globalization: Lessons from Asia*. Washington DC: Institute for International Economics.

Ocampo, José Antonio, Jan Kregel and Stephanie Griffith-Jones. 2007. *International Finance and Development*. London: Zed Books.

Ocampo, José Antonio and José Gabriel Palma. 2008. "The Role of Preventive Capital Account Regulations." In *Capital Market Liberalization and Development*, edited by José Antonio Ocampo and Joseph E. Stiglitz. New York: Oxford University Press. 170–204.

Ocampo, José Antonio and Maria Angela Parra. 2003. "The Terms of Trade for Commodities in the 20th Century." *CEPAL Review* 79: 7–35.

Ocampo, José Antonio, Shari Spiegel and Joseph E. Stiglitz. 2008. "Capital Market Liberalization and Development." In *Capital Market Liberalization and Development*, edited by José Antonio Ocampo and Joseph E. Stiglitz. New York: Oxford University Press. 1–47.

OECD. 1998. *Multilateral Agreement on Investment*. OECD. Online: http://www.oecd.org/docu ment/22/0,3343,en_2649_33783766_1894819_1_1_1_1,00.html (accessed September 2009).

———. 2004. "'Indirect Expropriation' and the 'Right to Regulate' in International Investment Law." Working Papers on International Investment Number 2004/4.

———. 2009. "Codes of Liberalization." Online: http://www.oecd.org/dataoecd/41/21/2030182.pdf (accessed September 2009).

Ohlin, Bertil G. 1967. *Interregional and International Trade*. Cambridge, MA: Harvard University Press.

Okimoto, Daniel. 1989. *Between MITI and the Market: Japanese Industrial Policy for High Technology*. Palo Alto: Stanford University Press.

Oxfam International. 2007. *All Costs, No Benefits: How TRIPS-Plus Intellectual Property Rules in the US–Jordan FTA Affect Access to Medicines*. London: Oxfam International.

Panagariya, Arvind. 1999. "The Regionalism Debate: An Overview." *World Economy* 22, no. 4: 455–76.

Panizza, Ugo. 2010. "Is Domestic Debt the Answer to Debt Crises?" In *Overcoming Developing Country Debt Crises*, edited by Barry Herman, José Antonio Ocampo and Shari Spiegel. New York: Oxford University Press. 91–108.

Peres, Wilson. 2006. "The Slow Comeback of Industrial Policies in Latin America and the Caribbean." *CEPAL Review* 88: 67–83.

Phillips, Nicola. 2005. "U.S. Power and the Politics of Economic Governance in the Americas." *Latin American Politics & Society* 47, no. 4: 1–25.

Polaski, Sandra. 2006. *Winners and Losers: Impact of the Doha Round on Developing Countries*. Washington DC: Carnegie Endowment for International Peace.

Porzecanski, Arturo C. 2005. "From Rogue Creditors to Rogue Debtors: Implications of Argentina's Default." *Chicago Journal of International Law* 6, no. 1: 311–32.

———. 2010. "Testimony, Hearing on the Argentine Bond Default and its Impact on New York State." New York State Senate Standing Committee on Banks, 23 April.

Prasad, Eswar, Kenneth Rogoff, Shang-Jin Wei and M. Ayhan Kose. 2003. "Effects of Financial Globalization on Developing Countries: Some Empirical Evidence." IMF Occasional Paper. Washington DC: International Monetary Fund.

Raghavan, Chakravarthi. 2009. "Financial Services, the WTO, and Initiatives for Global Financial Reform." G-24 Discussion Paper. New York: United Nations.

Ramírez, Marienella Ortiz. 2008. "El Perú logra allanar el camino para TLC con Estados Unidos." *ElComercio.com.pe*, 15 August. Online: http://www.elcomercio.com.pe/edicionimpresa/Html/2008-08-15/el-peru-logra-allanar-camino-tlc-estados-unidos.html (accessed September 2009).

Reinhart, Carmen and Kenneth Rogoff. 2009. *This Time is Different: Eight Centuries of Financial Folly*. Princeton: Princeton University Press.

Rhee, Yung Whee. 1985. "Instruments for Export Policy and Administration: Lessons from the East Asian Experience." World Bank Staff, Working Paper No. 725.

Ricardo, David. 1911. *On Principles of Political Economy and Taxation*. London: J. M. Dent & Sons.

Rodrik, Dani. 1992. "Conceptual Issues in the Design of Trade Policy for Industrialization." *World Development* 20, no. 3: 309–20.

_____. 2005. *Industrial Policy for the 21st Century*. Vienna: United Nations Industrial Development Organization.

_____. 2007. *One Economics, Many Recipes: Globalization, Institutions, and Economic Growth*. Princeton: Princeton University Press.

_____. 2008. "Normalizing Industrial Policy." Commission on Growth and Development, Working Paper No. 3.

_____. 2011. *The Globalization Paradox: Democracy and the Future of the World Economy*. New York: W. W. Norton & Co.

Rodrik, Dani and Arvind Subramanian. 2009. "Why Did Financial Globalization Disappoint?" *IMF Staff Papers* 56, no. 1: 112–38.

Rogoff, Kenneth and Jeromin Zettelmeyer. 2002. "Bankruptcy Procedures for Sovereigns: A History of Ideas, 1976–2001." IMF Working Paper No. 02/133. Washington DC: International Monetary Fund.

Roland-Holst, David and Dominique van der Mensbrugghe. 2002. "Regionalism versus Globalization in the Americas: Empirical Evidence on Opportunities and Challenges." Washington DC: World Bank.

Ruggie, J. G. 1983. "International Regimes, Transactions, and Change: Embedded Liberalism in the Postwar Economic Order." In *International Regimes*, edited by Stephen D. Krasner. Ithaca: Cornell University Press.

SAFTA (Agreement on South Asian Free Trade Area). 2004. 6 January. Online: http://www.saarc-sec.org/userfiles/saftaagreement.pdf (accessed 11 September 2012).

Salacuse, Jeswald. 2010. *The Law of Investment Treaties*. Oxford: Oxford University Press.

Salazar-Xirinachs, José. 2004. "The Proliferation of Regional Trade Agreements in the Americas: An Assessment of Key Issues." In *The Strategic Dynamics of Latin American Trade*, edited by Vinod K. Aggarwal, Ralph H. Espach and Joseph S. Tulchin. Palo Alto: Stanford University Press. 116–57.

Sargent, John and Linda Matthews. 2001. "Combining Export Processing Zones and Regional Free Trade Agreements: Lessons From the Mexican Experience." *World Development* 29, no. 10: 1739–52.

Schneider, Ben R. 2009. "Hierarchical Market Economies and Varieties of Capitalism in Latin America." *Journal of Latin American Studies* 41: 553–75.

Schrank, Andrew and Marcus J. Kurtz. 2005. "Credit Where Credit is Due: Open Economy Industrial Policy and Export Diversification in Latin America and the Caribbean." *Politics & Society* 33, no. 4: 671–702.

SCM (Agreement on Subsidies and Countervailing Measures). 1994. Marrakesh Agreement Establishing the World Trade Organization, Annex 1A, Legal Instruments – Results of the Uruguay Round, 15 April, 33 I.L.M. 1125.

Setser, Brad. 2010. "The Political Economy of the SDRM." In *Overcoming Developing Country Debt Crises*, edited by Barry Herman, José Antonio Ocampo and Shari Spiegel. New York: Oxford University Press. 317–46.

Shadlen, Kenneth C. 2004. *Democratization without Representation: The Politics of Small Industry in Mexico*. University Park: Pennsylvania State University Press.

_____. 2005a. "Exchanging Development for Market Access?: Deep Integration and Industrial Policy under Multilateral and Regional-Bilateral Trade Agreements." *Review of International Political Economy* 12, no. 5: 750–75.

_____. 2005b. "Policy Space for Development in the WTO and Beyond: The Case of Intellectual Property Rights." Global Development and Environment Institute, Working Paper No. 05–06.

_____. 2006. "Latin American Trade and Development in the New International Economy." *Latin American Research Review* 41, no. 3: 210–21.

_____. 2008. "Globalization, Power, and Integration: The Political Economy of Regional and Bilateral Trade Agreements in the Americas." *Journal of Development Studies* 44, no. 1: 1–20.

Siegel, Deborah. 2004. "Using Free Trade Agreements to Control Capital Account Restrictions: Summary of Remarks on the Relationship to the Mandate of the IMF." *ILSA Journal of International and Comparative Law* 297: 301–2.

South Centre. 2004. "Revenue Implications of WTO NAMA Tariff Reduction." South Centre analytical note.

Stanford, Jim. 2003. "Economic Models and Economic Reality." *International Journal of Political Economy* 33, no. 3: 28–49.

Stiglitz, Joseph E. and M. Shahe Emran. 2004. "Price Neutral Tax reform with an Informal Economy." Econometric Society 2004 North American Summer Meetings no. 493.

Stolper, Wolfgang F. and Paul A. Samuelson. 1941. "Protection and Real Wages." *Review of Economic Studies* 9, no. 1: 58–73.

Straus, Joseph. 2001. "The Present State of the Patent System in the European Union: As Compared with the Situation in the United States of America and Japan." Online: http://suepo.org/public/docs/2001/straus.pdf (accessed 11 September 2012).

Stumberg, Robert. 2009. *Reform of Investment Provisions.* Online: http://waysandmeans.house.gov/Hearings/Testimony.aspx?TID=2163 (accessed September 2010).

Sturzenegger, Federico and Jeromin Zettelmeyer. 2006. *Debt Defaults and Lessons from a Decade of Crisis.* Cambridge, MA: MIT Press.

Tanzi, Vito, Alberto Barreix and Luiz Villela, eds. 2008. *Taxation and Latin American Integration.* David Rockefeller Center for Latin American Studies, Harvard University/Inter-American Development Bank.

Thacker, Strom C. 2000. *Big Business, The State, and Free Trade: Constructing Coalitions in Mexico.* Cambridge: Cambridge University Press.

Thompson, Helen and David Runciman. 2006. "Sovereign Debt and Private Creditors: New Legal Sanction or the Enduring Power of States?" *New Political Economy* 11, no. 4: 541–55.

Thorstensen, Vera, Emerson Marçal and Lucas Ferraz. 2011. "Impacts of Exchange Rates on International Trade Policy Instruments: The Case of Tariffs." São Paulo School of Economics (EESP), FGV, September.

TRIMS. 1994. Agreement on Trade-Related Investment Measures, Annex, Marrakesh Agreement Establishing the World Trade Organization, Annex 1A, Legal Instruments – Results of the Uruguay Round, 15 April, 33 I.L.M. 1125.

TRIPS. 1994. Agreement on Trade-Related Aspects of Intellectual Property Rights, Marrakesh Agreement Establishing the World Trade Organization, Annex 1C, Legal Instruments – Results of the Uruguay Round, 15 April, 33 I.L.M. 1125.

Tucker, Todd and Lori Wallach. 2009. "No Meaningful Safeguards for Prudential Measures in World Trade Organization's Financial Service Deregulation Agreements." *Special Pittsburgh G-20 Report.* Washington DC: Public Citizen.

UNCTAD. *International Investment Agreement Database.* Online: http://unctad.org/en/pages/DIAE/International%20Investment%20Agreements%20%28IIA%29/IIA-Tools.aspx (accessed 6 July 2010).

United Nations. 2002. "Millennium Development Goals." New York: United Nations. Online: http://www.unctadxi.org/templates/DocSearch____779.aspx (accessed April 2010).

United States of America. 2004. Model Bilateral Investment Treaty. US Department of State.

US–Australia. 2004. U.S.–Australia Free Trade Agreement, U.S.–Australia, 18 May, 43 I.L.M. 1248.

US–Chile. 2003. U.S.–Chile Free Trade Agreement, U.S.–Chile, 6 June, 42 I.L.M. 1026.

US Department of State. 2003. Subcommittee on Domestic and International Monetary, Trade and Technology of the Committee on Financial Services in the US House of Representatives. *Hearing on Opening Trade in Financial Services—The Chile and Singapore Examples*, 1 April.

USDOS (United States Department of State). 2009. "Report of the Subcommittee on Investment of the Advisory Committee on International Economic Policy Regarding the Model Bilateral Investment Treaty." Advisory Committee on International Economic Policy. 2004 Model BIT, Washington DC. Online: http://www.state.gov/e/eeb/rls/othr/2009/131098.htm (accessed April 2010).

US House of Representatives. 2003. Hearing on Trade in Financial Services, Subcommittee on Domestic and International Monetary Policy, Trade and Technology Committee on Financial Services, US House of Representatives. Online: http://tinyurl.com/JTaylor-2003 (accessed 2 May 2013).

US–Morocco. 2004. U.S.–Morocco Free Trade Agreement, U.S.–Morocco, 15 June, 44 I.L.M. 544.

US–Peru. 2006. U.S.–Peru Trade Promotion Agreement, U.S.–Peru, 12 April. Online: http://www.ustr.gov/Trade_Agreements/Bilateral/Peru_TPA/Final_Texts/Section_Index.html (accessed 11 September 2012).

US–Singapore. 2003. U.S.–Singapore Free Trade Agreement, U.S.–Sing., 6 May, 42 I.L.M. 1026.

Valckx, Nico. 2002. "WTO Financial Services Commitments: Determinants and Impact on Financial Stability." IMF Working Paper WP/02/214. Washington DC: International Monetary Fund.

Van Aaken, Anne and Jürgen Kurtz. 2009. "Prudence or Discrimination?: Emergency Measures, the Global Financial Crisis, and International Economic Law." *Journal of International Economic Law* 12, no. 4: 859–94.

Van Harten, Gus. 2009. "Reforming the NAFTA Investment Regime." In *The Future of North American Trade Policy: Lessons from NAFTA (A Task Force Report)*, edited by Kevin P. Gallagher, Enrique Dussel Peters and Timothy A. Wise. Boston: Frederick S. Pardee Center for the Study of the Longer-Range Future. 43–52.

Vandevelde, Kenneth J. 2008. *US International Investment Agreements*. Oxford: Oxford University Press.

Wade, Robert. 2004a. *Governing the Market: Economic Theory and the Role of Government in East Asian Industrialization*. Princeton: Princeton University Press.

_____. 2004b. "Is Globalization Reducing Poverty and Inequality?" *World Development* 32, no. 4: 567–89.

Waibel, Michael. 2007. "Opening Pandora's Box: Sovereign Bonds in International Arbitration." *American Journal of International Law* 101, no. 4: 711–59.

_____. 2011. *Sovereign Defaults before International Courts and Tribunals*. Cambridge: Cambridge University Press.

Weiss, John. 2005. "Export Growth and Industrial Policy: Lessons from the East Asian Miracle Experience." Asian Development Bank Institute, Discussion Paper No. 26.

Wells, Louis T. 2010. "Property Rights for Foreign Capital: Sovereign Debt and Private Direct Investment in Times of Crisis." In *The Yearbook on International Investment Law and Policy 2009–2010*, edited by Karl Sauvant. Oxford: Oxford University Press. 477–504.

Winters, L. Alan, Terrie Walmsley, Zhen Kun Wang and Roman Grynberg. 2003. "Liberalizing Temporary Movement of Natural Persons: An Agenda for the Development Round." *World Economy* 26, no. 8: 1137–61.

Wise, C. and M. Pastor. 1994. "The Origins and Sustainability of Mexico's Free Trade Policy." *International Organization* 48: 459–89

Wise, Timothy A. and Kevin P. Gallagher. 2008. "Back to the Drawing Board: No Basis for Concluding the Doha Round of Negotiations." RIS Policy Brief no. 36, April, Delhi.

World Bank. 2010. Quarterly External Debt Statistics. Washington DC: World Bank. Online: http://web.worldbank.org/wbsite/external/datastatistics/extdecweds/0,,menuPK:1805431~pagePK:64168427~piPK:64168435~theSitePK:1805415,00.html (accessed July 2010).

_____. 1993. *The East Asian Miracle: Economic Growth and Public Policy.* New York: Oxford University Press.

_____. 2002. *Global Economic Prospects.* Washington DC: World Bank.

_____. 2005. *Global Economic Prospects: Trade, Regionalism, and Development.* Washington DC: World Bank.

_____. 2008. *World Development Indicators.* Washington DC: World Bank.

Woo-Cumings, Meredith. 1999. *The Developmental State: Cornell Studies in Political Economy.* Ithaca: Cornell University Press.

WTO (World Trade Organization). 2001. Declaration on the TRIPS Agreement and Public Health. WT/MIN(01)/DEC/2. Online: http://www.wto.org/english/thewto_e/minist_e/min01_e/mindecl_trips_e.htm (accessed 12 September 2012).

_____. 2010a. Financial Services: Background Note by the Secretariat. S/C/W/312/S/FIN/W/73. Geneva: World Trade Organization.

_____. 2010b. Chile: Tariff Profile. Online: http://stat.wto.org/TariffProfiles/CL_e.htm (accessed 12 September 2012).

_____. 2012a. Current Situations of Schedules of WTO Members, 12 April. Online: http://www.wto.org/english/tratop_e/schedules_e/goods_schedules_table_e.htm (accessed 12 September 2012).

_____. 2012b. WTO Legal Texts. Online: http://www.wto.org/english/docs_e/legal_e/legal_e.htm (accessed 12 September 2012).

Zoellick, Robert. 2005. *USTR 2005 Trade Policy Agenda.* United States Trade Representative, Government Printing Office.

INDEX

www.ingramcontent.com/pod-product-compliance
Lightning Source LLC
Chambersburg PA
CBHW020001290326
41935CB00007B/257